4 HUNGRY
College Boys

101 RECIPES FOR WHEN
MOM STOPS COOKING

For Gabe, Newm, and Nick…without you none of this would be possible.

A big thank you to all who helped me along the way, your time and patience are invaluable

Patricia Newman

Leigh Wysocki

Marcy Wysocki

Selina Wagner

Table of Contents

To successfully create <u>EVERY</u> dish within this book, there are certain tools that are required...

- 6 Qt. slow cooker
- 6 Qt. pot (Dutch oven)
- 3 Qt. saucepan
- 12" stainless steel frying pan
- 12" non-stick frying pan
- 10-inch cast-iron skillet
- Chef's knife
- Tongs
- Small, Medium, and Large mixing bowls
- Colander
- Liquid cup measure
- Dry cup measure (1/8 C – 1 C)
- Measuring spoons (1/4 t – 1 T)
- Meat thermometer
- Can opener
- Microwave
- Toaster
- Oven
- Stovetop
- Waffle iron
- Standard Blender
- Cutting board
- 9-inch pie plate
- 8x8 baking dish
- Loaf pan
- Jelly roll pan
- Baking sheet
- 9x13 oven safe dish
- Pasta spoon
- Mixing spatula
- Spatula
- Whisk

- Peeler
- Grater
- Meat tenderizer

There are also optional tools...

- 3 cup rice cooker
- Panini press
- Slow cooker liners
- Handheld Mixer (to replace whisking by hand)

CH. 1 POULTRY

4

Sweet and Sour Chicken

Serves 4 Hungry College Boys
Prep Time: ~25 min
Total Time: 1 hour

Ingredients

1 C rice, any variety
2 C water
Olive oil
2 lb. boneless skinless chicken breasts, cut into 1-inch
        cubes
Salt
Pepper
1 T garlic powder
1 C zucchini, cut into 1/2-inch cubes
1 C yellow squash, cut into 1/2-inch cubes
1/2 C onion, chopped
12 oz. Asian vegetable mix, frozen or fresh
2/3 C sweet and sour sauce
Unsalted cashews (optional)

Directions

Pour the rice and water into a rice cooker* and turn on
cooker. Drizzle olive oil into a large pan and turn the
burner to medium-high heat. Once the oil begins to
smoke, toss in chicken. Season generously with the salt,
pepper, and garlic. Brown the chicken for 6-8 minutes,
stirring occasionally, or until internal temperature reaches
165°. Remove the chicken and all excess juice from the
pan and set aside. Toss in all vegetables and season with
salt and pepper to taste. Sauté the vegetables for 8-10
minutes, stirring often, and add back the chicken and
juices. Pour Sweet and Sour sauce into your pan and stir
to combine. Turn heat down to medium-low and allow
mixture to simmer for another 5-7 minutes, stirring often.
Serve in bowls with the rice. Top with cashews if desired.

*For cooking without a rice cooker:
- Cook according to package directions

6

Primavera Stuffed Chicken

Serves 4 Hungry College Boys
Prep Time: ~30 min
Total Time: 1 hour 5 min

Ingredients

Balsamic vinaigrette
1-1/2 C panko bread crumbs
1 T complete seasoning
4 boneless skinless chicken breasts, butterflied and
       tenderized thin (1/4-1/8 in.)
1 zucchini, sliced thin
1/2 C red onion, sliced thin
1 tomato, sliced thin
1 eggplant, sliced thin
Toothpicks
1/4 C grated parmesan
Balsamic vinegar

Directions

Preheat oven to 400°. Prepare a coating station with one plate filled with balsamic vinaigrette and another with bread crumbs mixed with complete seasoning. Dredge chicken through the vinaigrette, then the bread crumbs, and place on a baking sheet. Stuff chicken with sliced vegetables, in any order you choose, and secure shut with toothpicks. Sprinkle grated parmesan over the top of each breast. Bake chicken 25-40 minutes or until internal temperature reaches 165°. Let chicken rest 2-3 minutes, then serve with a drizzle of balsamic vinegar on top.

8

Chicken Quesadilla

Serves 4 Hungry College Boys
Prep Time: ~25 min
Total Time: 45 min

Ingredients

Olive oil
Salt
Pepper
1 C yellow onion, sliced thin
8 oz. mushrooms, sliced thin
Butter
4 large flour tortillas
4 C (16 oz.) four cheese Mexican blend
1 mojo rotisserie chicken, shredded
8 oz. can sweet corn, drained
1/2 C grape tomatoes, chopped
Sour cream
Salsa

Directions

In a pan, drizzle olive oil and turn burner to medium heat. Toss onions in pan, season with salt and pepper, then sauté for 8-10 minutes or until onions are caramel in color. Set aside. In the same pan, drizzle olive oil and sauté mushrooms for 6-8 minutes until excess moisture has cooked off and mushrooms are slightly browned, set aside. Lightly butter one side of the tortilla, then place butter side down in the same pan over medium heat. Layer cheese, chicken, corn, onions, and mushrooms to liking on half of the tortilla, then top with cheese. Fold over tortilla and let cook 1-2 minutes per side or until tortilla has browned on both sides and cheese has melted. Serve by topping with sour cream and salsa.

10

Slow Cooker Jerk Chicken with Caribbean Black Beans

Serves 4 Hungry College Boys
Prep Time: ~20 min
Total Time: 4 hours 15 min

Ingredients

2 T canola oil
1/4 C brown sugar
1/3 C soy sauce
2 T minced garlic
2 T pureed ginger
1 T cinnamon
1 t allspice
1 t dried thyme
1/4 t nutmeg
1 medium jalapeño, stem and seeds removed (serrano for more heat)
1 medium navel orange, cut into 1/4-inch slices
1 medium yellow onion, cut into wedges
4 boneless skinless chicken breasts
1 C rice, uncooked
2 C water
16 oz. can seasoned black beans
8 oz. can corn, drained

Directions

In a blender, blend together the oil, brown sugar, soy sauce, garlic, ginger, cinnamon, allspice, thyme, nutmeg, and jalapeño until even consistency. Place the orange and the onions along the bottom of the slow cooker. Place chicken on top of orange and onion, then pour 2/3 of the spice rub on the chicken, making sure to coat thoroughly with hands. Save the remaining third of spice rub. Cook on high for 4 hours. When 30 minutes are remaining on the chicken, combine rice with water in a rice cooker* and start the cooker. Preheat oven to broil. In a separate pot, combine black beans and corn, and turn burner to medium heat. Place chicken on a foil-lined baking sheet and pour remaining spice rub over the top of the chicken. Broil

11

chicken for 5 minutes, watching carefully to make sure not to burn. Remove chicken once a nice crust has formed. Once rice has finished cooking, combine with black beans and corn, mixing to incorporate. Serve with orange and onion from slow cooker and spoon juice from slow cooker over rice.

*For cooking without a rice cooker:
- Cook according to package directions

Sun Dried Tomato Pesto Chicken Panini

Serves 4 Hungry College Boys
Prep Time: ~20 min
Total Time: 30 min

Ingredients

1 T olive oil
4 boneless skinless chicken breasts, cut in half lengthwise
1 t salt
1 t pepper
1 t garlic powder
1/2 t red pepper flakes
1 loaf sourdough bread, sliced
8 t mayonnaise
8 oz. sun dried tomato pesto
1 tomato, sliced
1 head of romaine, chopped into sandwich size pieces
8 slices of provolone

Directions

Drizzle olive oil in a pan and turn burner to medium-high heat. Season chicken cutlets with the salt, pepper, garlic, and red pepper flakes. Brown chicken cutlets for 4-5 minutes a side, cooking for 10 minutes total or until internal temp reaches 165°, then set aside. Preheat Panini maker* to high heat or equivalent. Spread 1 t mayonnaise on one side of each piece of bread. Place mayonnaise sides down and spread 1 T sun dried tomato pesto on each piece of bread. Place two slices of tomato on one slice of bread, then two chicken cutlets, two slices of provolone, three pieces of romaine, and close with the other slice of bread. Cook in panini griddle for 5-7 minutes or until nice dark panini press marks have formed and the cheese has melted. Cut as desired and serve.

*for cooking on non-stick pan
- Preheat pan with burner at medium-high heat. Place sandwich on pan and press flat

13

with a spatula. Cook for 2-3 minutes per side. Bread should have a brown crisp edge and cheese should be melted. Watch carefully to not burn sandwich.

15

16

"Fried" Chicken and Waffles

Serves 4 Hungry College Boys
Prep Time: ~20 min
Total Time: 1 hour

Ingredients

2 large eggs
1/4 C whole milk
1 T salt, divided
1 T pepper, divided
1/4 t allspice
1 t garlic powder
4 boneless skinless chicken breasts, patted dry
3-1/2 C Frosted Flakes, crushed
Cooking spray
8 frozen waffles
Maple syrup

Directions

Preheat oven to 350° and arrange oven rack 4-6 inches from top heating element. In a bowl, whisk together the eggs and milk. Season chicken with 1/2 T salt, 1/2 T pepper, allspice and garlic powder. Combine the remaining salt and pepper with the frosted flakes in a large bowl, then create a breading assembly line. Dip chicken in egg mixture, covering completely, then coat with the frosted flakes using your hand to press down and add as much breading as possible, then place on greased cookie sheet. Once chicken is thoroughly coated in breading, use the cooking spray to give a quick spray on top of the chicken. Place in oven and bake for 25-40 minutes depending on the size and thickness of the breast or until internal temperature is 165°. Leave chicken in oven when timer ends and turn oven to broil for 5 minutes. In the last 5 minutes, toast the waffles for 4-5 minutes. Serve with a generous drizzle of maple syrup.

18

Slow Cooker BBQ Chicken Sandwich and Cornbread

Serves 4 Hungry College Boys
Prep Time: ~20 min
Total Time: 6-8 hours

Ingredients

1 red onion, chopped into wedges
4 boneless skinless chicken breasts
1 t garlic powder
1 t ground cumin
1/2 t smoked paprika
1 t salt
1 t black pepper
10 oz. BBQ sauce
15 oz. box cornbread mix
1 egg
1 C whole milk
1/4 C vegetable oil
15 oz. can cream corn
1 T butter, melted
Honey
4 potato rolls

Directions

Place onions at the bottom of the crock pot and place chicken breasts on top. Season chicken breasts with garlic powder, cumin, smoked paprika, salt, and pepper. Pour BBQ sauce over the chicken and coat each breast entirely. Cook covered on low for 6-8 hours. Shred chicken with forks and leave warm while preparing cornbread. Preheat oven according to cornbread mix directions. In a bowl combine the cornbread mix, egg, milk, oil and cream corn. When thoroughly incorporated into a pancake-like batter, pour into an oven-safe 9x9 or 8x8 pan. Bake for 25-30 minutes or until a toothpick in the center comes out clean. Place cornbread on cooling rack and brush butter on top. Let cool for 2-3 minutes then serve topped with honey. Place chicken on potato rolls when serving.

19

20

Savory Pumpkin Pancakes with Maple-Balsamic Salad and Sausage

Serves 4 Hungry College Boys
Prep Time: ~20 min
Total Time: 1 hour

Ingredients

Canola oil
1 lb. turkey sausage, remove from casing
1 C onion, finely chopped
2 t dried rosemary
1-1/2 t minced garlic
1 C all-purpose flour
1/2 t salt
1/2 t baking powder
1/4 t baking soda
1/4 t pepper
2 large eggs
1/2 C pumpkin puree
2 T honey
2 T apple cider vinegar
3 oz. milk
1 C (4 oz.) shredded cheddar
1/2 C balsamic vinaigrette
2 T maple syrup
1 T stone ground mustard
5 oz. spring salad mix

Directions

Drizzle canola oil in a pan and turn burner to medium heat. Brown sausage for 8-10 minutes then set aside in a paper towel-lined bowl to absorb the excess grease. Sauté onion for 6-8 minutes. Add rosemary and garlic and cook for an additional 2-3 minutes. Set aside. In a large bowl, whisk together flour, salt, baking powder, baking soda, and pepper. Add the eggs, pumpkin, honey, vinegar, milk, and onion mixture. Mix to combine, then fold in cheddar. Drizzle canola oil on a non-stick pan on medium heat. Pour batter into silver-dollar size pancakes and cook on each side 2-3 minutes (bubbles should form and be popped). Batter should make 8-9 thick pancakes. In a small bowl whisk to combine the balsamic, maple syrup, and mustard, until homogenous. Pour dressing over salad then add sausage and toss to combine. Serve pancakes with salad on the side.

Slow Cooker Chicken Curry

Serves 4 Hungry College Boys
Prep Time: ~40 min
Total Time: 6-8 hours

Ingredients

Olive oil
1 C onion, diced
2 t minced garlic
4 boneless skinless chicken breasts
3 stalks of celery, diced
4 medium carrots, sliced into small pieces
15 oz. can sweet peas, drained
2 lb. baby potatoes, cut into bite size pieces
2 14 oz. cans coconut milk
1-1/2 T pureed fresh ginger
1-1/2 T curry powder
1/2 t cayenne
2 T soy sauce
1/2 C reduced sodium chicken stock
1 t salt
1/2 t pepper
1 C rice, uncooked
2 C water

Directions

Drizzle olive oil in a pan and turn the burner to medium heat. Sauté onions for 4-6 minutes, then add the garlic and cook an additional two minutes, stirring occasionally. Remove from heat and set aside. Place the chicken breasts at the bottom of the slow cooker, then add the onion mixture, celery, carrots, peas, potatoes, coconut milk, ginger, curry powder, cayenne, soy sauce, chicken stock, salt, and pepper. Mix to combine. Cook covered on low for 6-8 hours, stirring every 2 hours. About an hour before serving, begin cooking the rice*. Place rice in rice cooker and add 2 C water. Shred chicken and serve over rice.

*For cooking without a rice cooker:
- Cook according to package directions

26

Spinach and Artichoke Dip Stuffed Chicken

Serves 4 Hungry College Boys
Prep Time: ~25 min
Total Time: 50 min

Ingredients

4 boneless skinless chicken breasts, butterflied
9 oz. frozen chopped spinach, thawed and drained
9 oz. spinach and artichoke dip
2 T olive oil
1/2 t salt
1/4 t pepper
1/4 t garlic powder
Dash of nutmeg

Directions

Preheat oven to 400°. On a baking sheet, tenderize and flatten the chicken to 1/2-inch thickness. In a bowl, combine spinach and spinach dip and mix until uniform consistency. Place 2 tablespoon-sized dollops of the spinach mixture in the center of each breast until no mixture remains and fold over on top of itself. (Optional: secure chicken closed with toothpicks). In a small bowl, combine olive oil, salt, pepper, garlic powder, and nutmeg. Spoon the oil mixture over the top of each breast and spread until top is coated. Bake chicken for 25-40 minutes or until internal temperature reaches 165°. Let chicken rest 5 minutes before serving.

28

Buffalo Chicken Tacos

Serves 4 Hungry College Boys
Prep Time: ~10 min
Total Time: 30 min

Ingredients

4 boneless skinless chicken breasts
1/2 t garlic powder
1 t salt
1/2 t pepper
6 oz. broccoli slaw
4 celery stalks, finely chopped
Blue cheese dressing
2/3 C buffalo sauce
12 corn tortillas

Directions

Preheat oven to 400°. Season chicken breasts with garlic, salt, and pepper. Place on a greased cookie sheet and bake for 25-40 minutes depending on size of the breast or until internal temperature reaches 165°. In a medium bowl, mix half of the broccoli slaw, celery, and 1/4 C of blue cheese dressing. Add more dressing as desired. When chicken is done cooking, place all breasts in a large bowl and shred. Pour buffalo sauce over the chicken and toss to coat evenly. Serve by placing chicken on tortillas and top with slaw.

30

Slow Cooker Corn Chowder

Serves 4 Hungry College Boys
Prep Time: ~10 min
Total Time: 7-8 hours

Ingredients

2 lb. smoked turkey sausage or kielbasa smoked sausage,
      sliced into 1/2-inch rounds
4 C reduced sodium chicken broth
3 medium-sized russet potatoes, washed and cut into bite
      size pieces
15 oz. can whole kernel corn
15 oz. can cream corn
2 medium poblano peppers, seeds removed and finely
      chopped
1 t salt
1/2 t pepper
1 C heavy cream
Cayenne pepper (optional)

Directions

In a slow cooker add the sausage, chicken broth, potatoes,
corn, cream corn, poblano peppers, salt, and pepper.
Cook covered on low for 7-8 hours and mix in the cream
before serving. (optional) Sprinkle a dash of cayenne over
top for added heat if desired.

32

Buffalo Chicken Stuffed Sweet Potatoes

Serves 4 Hungry College Boys
Prep Time: ~10 min
Total Time: 1 hour

Ingredients

Olive oil
4 medium sweet potatoes
4 boneless skinless chicken breasts
1/2 t salt
1/4 t pepper
1/4 t garlic powder
2/3 C buffalo sauce
Blue cheese crumbles
Blue cheese dressing

Directions

Preheat oven to 400°. Coat sweet potatoes with oil, pierce with fork, then wrap tightly in foil. Bake for 1 hour or until soft. On a greased baking sheet place chicken breasts. Season chicken with 1/2 t salt, 1/4 t pepper, and 1/4 t garlic powder. Bake for 25-40 minutes, depending on size or until internal temperature reaches 165°. Remove chicken from oven and shred in a large bowl. Pour buffalo sauce on the chicken and toss to combine. Remove potatoes from oven and cut lengthwise down the center. Fill with chicken. Top with blue cheese crumbles and drizzle blue cheese dressing as desired.

34

Stuffing Waffles with Turkey Breast, Cranberry Sauce, and Gravy

Serves 4 Hungry College Boys
Prep Time: ~10 min
Total Time: 1 hour

Ingredients

1 lb. Italian sausage, remove from casing
1-1/4 t ground dried sage, divided
1 t dried thyme, divided
1/2 t dried rosemary
1/2 t black pepper, divided
1/4 t ground nutmeg
2 celery stalks, finely chopped
1/2 C onion, finely chopped
2 3/4 lb. turkey breasts, cut in half lengthwise
14 oz. herbed seasoned bread stuffing
2 C reduced sodium chicken broth
2 large eggs
1/4 t garlic powder
1/2 t salt
1 T butter, divided into 4 pats
12 oz. turkey gravy
14 oz. can whole berry cranberry sauce

Directions

Preheat oven to 400°. Place a pan on a burner and turn to medium heat. Brown sausage for 6-8 minutes then add 1 t sage, 3/4 t thyme, 1/2 t rosemary, 1/4 t pepper, and 1/4 t nutmeg. Spread sausage to the outside of the pan and add the celery and onion, then cook an additional 10-12 minutes, stirring frequently. Line a large bowl with paper towels and empty contents of pan into bowl to drain some of the fat. In a large mixing bowl add the dried stuffing mix, sausage mixture, chicken broth, and eggs then mix to combine. Place turkey on a greased baking sheet and season both sides with garlic powder, salt, 1/4 t sage, and 1/4 t thyme. Place a pat of butter on top of each breast and bake for 28-30 minutes or until internal temperature reaches 165°. Preheat and grease a waffle iron. Using a

35

1/4 C dry measuring cup, take a rounded scoop of stuffing mixture and evenly spread on waffle iron. Cook for 2-3 minutes or until timer on waffle maker goes off. Repeat until stuffing mix is used up. When turkey is done, let rest for 3-4 minutes. Heat gravy in microwave for 1 minute. Place cranberry sauce in a small bowl. Serve by drizzling gravy over turkey and waffles and top waffles with cranberry sauce if desired.

Cajun Spaghetti Squash Bake

Serves 4 Hungry College Boys
Prep Time: ~20 min
Total Time: 1 hour 30 min

Ingredients

2 T olive oil, divided
2 medium spaghetti squashes, seeds removed and halved
     lengthwise
3/4 t salt, divided
1/2 t pepper, divided
1 C all-purpose flour
4 boneless skinless chicken breasts, cut into 1-inch cubes
1 T creole seasoning
1 C onion, chopped
1 T minced garlic
1 red bell pepper, chopped
1 green bell pepper, chopped
2 oz. reduced-fat cream cheese
14 oz. can petite diced tomatoes, drained
Grated parmesan
Dried parsley

Directions

Preheat oven to 350°. Place spaghetti squash cut side up and rub 1/2 T olive oil on each half, then season with 1/4 t salt and 1/8 t pepper. Bake for 40 minutes or until easily pierced by a fork then set aside to cool. While squash bakes, in a bowl, combine flour, 1/2 t salt, 3/8 t pepper and mix to combine. Dredge chicken in flour. Drizzle 1 T olive in a pan and turn burner to slightly higher than medium heat. Add chicken to pan and season with 1 T creole seasoning. Brown chicken for 8-10 minutes then set aside. In the same pan reduce heat to medium and add onion. Sauté for 5-6 minutes then add the garlic and cook an additional 2-3 minutes. Add the peppers and cook for 5-6 minutes then add the cream cheese, tomatoes, chicken and mix to combine scraping the bottom of the pan. Empty contents of pan into an oven safe casserole dish. Using a fork, scrape the inside of the squashes into the casserole

37

dish. Mix to combine ingredients and bake for 20 minutes or until edges are brown and crispy. Serve by topping with grated parmesan and parsley.

39

40

Slow Cooker Turkey and Butternut Squash Chili

Serves 4 Hungry College Boys
Prep Time: ~10 min
Total Time: 1 hour

Ingredients

1 T olive oil
2 lb. ground turkey
1 C onion, chopped
2 t minced garlic
1/4 C chili powder
1 T ground cumin
1 t salt
1/2 t pepper
2 t ground coriander
14 oz. can petite diced tomatoes, drained
4 T tomato paste
2-1/2 T apple cider vinegar
2 14 oz. cans seasoned red beans
1 small butternut squash, peeled, seeded and chopped
        into 1/2-inch cubes
4 C water
Sour cream
Shredded cheddar cheese

Directions

Drizzle olive oil in a pan and turn burner to medium heat. Brown turkey for 8-10 minutes then spread to the outside of the pan and add onion and garlic. Sauté for an additional 5-7 minutes, stirring occasionally. Drain excess fat. Return pan to heat and add the chili powder, cumin, salt, pepper and coriander, mixing to combine. Add the tomatoes, tomato paste, and apple cider vinegar, and mix for about 1-2 minutes. Empty contents of pan into slow cooker and add the beans, butternut squash, and water, then mix to combine. Cook covered on low for 4-6 hours. Serve topped with a dollop of sour cream and shredded cheddar.

42

Grilled Rosemary Chicken with Orange Marmalade

Serves 4 Hungry College Boys
Prep Time: ~20 min
Total Time: 40 min

Ingredients

2 t salt
1 t pepper
4 t packed brown sugar
2-1/3 T minced fresh rosemary, divided
2-1/2 lb. boneless skinless chicken thighs, excess fat
        trimmed
2 T canola oil
1 C orange marmalade
1/4 C rice vinegar

Directions

In a small bowl, mix together the salt, pepper, brown sugar, and 2 T rosemary. Arrange chicken thighs on a baking sheet and drizzle with canola oil. Sprinkle mixture onto chicken and coat evenly with hands. Preheat grill to 425°. In a saucepan, combine the marmalade, 1/3 T rosemary, and rice vinegar. Turn burner to medium heat. When marmalade begins to bubble, stir occasionally and cook for 5-6 minutes until it has reduced by 1/3, then turn heat to low to keep warm. Place thighs on the grill and cook for 3-4 minutes per side. Let chicken rest for 3-5 minutes. Serve by pouring marmalade on top of chicken.

43

44

Thanksgiving Quesadillas

Serves 4 Hungry College Boys
Prep Time: ~10 min
Total Time: 6 hours

Ingredients

2 3/4 lb. turkey breasts
1/2 C chicken broth
2 T butter, melted
1/2 t thyme
1/2 t rosemary
1/2 t ground sage
1/4 t ground nutmeg
1/4 t pepper
4 large tortillas
4 C Wysocki Stuffing*
1 C (4 oz.) shredded cheddar, divided
14 oz. green beans, cooked
14 oz. can whole berry cranberry sauce
1-1/2 C turkey gravy

Directions

In a slow cooker add the turkey breasts and chicken broth. In a bowl combine melted butter with thyme, rosemary, ground sage, nutmeg, and pepper. Pour poultry seasoned butter over the turkey and cook covered on low for 4-6 hours. Once turkey is cooked, shred using forks. In a pan lay a large tortilla and turn the burner to medium heat. Arrange on each tortilla, 1/8 C cheddar, stuffing, green beans, turkey, cranberry sauce, then finish with 1/8 C cheddar and fold in half. Cook for 2-3 minutes per side. Heat gravy. Serve with a drizzle of gravy on top.

*See Page 187 for Wysocki Stuffing Recipe

46

Honey-Lime Sweet Potato and Spinach Salad

Serves 4 Hungry College Boys
Prep Time: ~15 min
Total Time: 45 min

Ingredients

3 medium sweet potatoes, peeled and sliced into 1/4-inch
        rounds
3 T olive oil, divided
1-1/2 t salt, divided
3/4 t pepper divided
1/2 t cumin
1/2 t smoked paprika
1/4 t garlic powder
1/4 t ground coriander
4 boneless skinless chicken breasts
1 t dried thyme
1 t dried rosemary
9 oz. fresh spinach
1 C matchstick carrots
For salad dressing
1/4 C canola oil
2 T honey
Dash of cayenne powder
1 T lime juice

Directions

Preheat oven to 425°. Lay out sliced sweet potatoes on a greased baking sheet then drizzle with 2 T olive oil. Sprinkle across sweet potatoes 1 t salt, 1/2 t pepper, cumin, smoked paprika, garlic powder, and coriander. Toss sweet potatoes until evenly coated in spices. Bake for 30 minutes, flipping after 15 minutes, potatoes should be fork tender. On a greased baking sheet drizzle 1 T olive oil over the chicken breasts and season with 1/2 t salt, 1/4 t pepper, thyme, and rosemary. Bake at 400° for 25-40 minutes depending on the size of the breasts or until internal temperature reaches 165°. Let chicken rest for 4-5 minutes then cut into bite size pieces. In a small mixing

47

bowl combine the canola oil, honey, cayenne, and lime juice. Place spinach and carrots on plate then top with sweet potatoes, chicken, and dressing.

Knock off Chipotle Chicken Bowl

Serves 4 Hungry College Boys
Prep Time: ~10 min
Total Time: 50 min

Ingredients

1-1/2 C white rice, dry
3 C water
4 T olive oil, divided
1 medium onion, sliced thin
1 green bell pepper, sliced thin
3/4 t garlic powder, divided
3/4 t chili powder, divided
1-1/2 t cumin, divided
2-1/2 t salt, divided
3/4 t pepper, divided
1/4 t cayenne, divided
~2 lb. boneless skinless chicken breasts, cut into 1-inch
        cubes
2 T lime juice
1/2 C corn, cooked
1/4 C fresh cilantro, chopped
Salsa
Sour cream

Directions

Pour the rice and water into a rice cooker* and turn on cooker. In a large pan drizzle 2 T of olive oil and turn burner to medium heat. Add the onions and bell pepper and season with 1/4 t garlic powder, 1/4 t chili powder, 1/2 t cumin, 1/2 t salt, 1/4 t pepper, and a dash of cayenne. Stir the vegetables often and let cook for 12-15 minutes or until tender. In a separate large pan drizzle 2 T of olive oil and turn burner to medium heat. Add the chicken and season with 1/2 t garlic powder, 1/2 t chili powder, 1 t cumin, 2 t salt, 1/2 t pepper, and a 1/4 t of cayenne. Allow the chicken to brown for 2 minutes then stir occasionally for 12-15 minutes or until no longer pink. Once the rice has finished cooking add the lime juice, corn, and cilantro and mix to combine. Serve chicken and vegetables over rice and top with salsa and sour cream.

*For cooking without a rice cooker:
- Cook according to package directions

51

52

Chicken Salad Sandwich

Serves 4 Hungry College Boys
Prep Time: ~25 min
Total Time: 30 min

Ingredients

1 rotisserie chicken, shredded
~6 oz. nonfat plain Greek yogurt
1 T dijon mustard
1 T mayonnaise
1 C fuji apple, diced
1 C red grapes, quartered
3 stalks of celery, diced
1 t dried tarragon
1/2 C walnuts, chopped
1/2 t salt
1/4 t pepper
1 large baguette
1 tomato, cut into 1/4-inch slices
1 head of romaine, chopped into sandwich size pieces

Directions

In a large mixing bowl combine the chicken, Greek yogurt, mustard, mayonnaise, apple, grapes, celery, tarragon, walnuts, salt, and pepper. Stir until even consistency and ingredients are spread throughout. Cut baguette into quarters and slice in half. Place tomato and lettuce on the base and fill with chicken salad.

54

Slow Cooker Pineapple Chicken

Serves 4 Hungry College Boys
Prep Time: ~10 min
Total Time: 6-8 hours

Ingredients

4 boneless skinless chicken breasts
1/2 C reduced sodium chicken broth
1/4 C brown sugar
3 T reduced sodium soy sauce
2 t minced garlic
20 oz. can of pineapple chunks in juice
2 T cornstarch
2 8-1/2 oz. packages precooked white rice
Sesame seeds
Dried parsley

Directions

Place chicken breasts at the bottom of the slow cooker. Combine in a mixing bowl the chicken broth, brown sugar, soy sauce, and minced garlic and stir to combine. Pour mixture over the chicken breasts and empty contents of pineapple chunks can into slow cooker. Cook covered on low for 6-8 hours then shred chicken. Mix together cornstarch and water and stir into chicken, then cook covered on high an additional 30 minutes. Cook rice in microwave according to package directions when ready to serve. Garnish with sesame seeds and parsley.

56

Chicken Caprese Salad

Serves 4 Hungry College Boys
Prep Time: ~15 min
Total Time: 30 min

Ingredients

4 boneless skinless chicken breasts
1/2 t salt.
1/4 t pepper
1/4 t garlic powder
1/2 t oregano
1/4 t dried parsley
5 oz. arugula
9 oz. grape tomatoes, halved
8 oz. mozzarella pearls
3/4 oz. fresh basil, chopped
Croutons
Balsamic vinaigrette
Balsamic glaze

Directions

*Preheat grill to 450°. Season both sides of the chicken with the salt, pepper, garlic powder, dried oregano, and dried parsley. Place chicken breast on the grates and cook for 6-7 minutes per side. Remove chicken from grill and let rest 2-3 minutes then chop into bite size pieces. Serve by placing arugula on the plate followed by the tomatoes, mozzarella, basil, croutons, and chicken. Then add balsamic vinaigrette as desired and finish with a quick drizzle of balsamic glaze.

*For cooking on pan

- Add 1 T olive oil and turn the burner to medium-high. When the oil begins to sizzle, or smoke, place the chicken in the pan. Cook for 6-8 minutes per side or until internal temp reaches 165°.

57

58

Peanut Lettuce Wraps

Serves 4 Hungry College Boys
Prep Time: ~10 min
Total Time: 45 min

Ingredients

1/3 C reduced sodium teriyaki sauce
3 T creamy peanut butter
1 T rice vinegar
1 T sesame oil
1/2 t salt
1/4 t pepper
2 lb. ground turkey
1/2 C matchstick carrots
2 t minced garlic
2 T pureed ginger
8 oz. water chestnuts, drained and diced
4 green onions, chopped
8 oz. snow peas
1 head of iceberg lettuce, ripped into bibs

Directions

In a mixing bowl add the teriyaki, peanut butter, rice vinegar, sesame oil, salt, and pepper. Whisk to combine ingredients and set aside. Place a large pan on a burner at medium heat. Add ground turkey and carrots into pan and cook for 8-12 minutes or until meat is no longer pink. Add garlic and ginger to pan and cook for 3-4 minutes stirring to incorporate. Pour sauce mixture into pan as well as the chestnuts and green onion then stir to combine cooking for 4-5 minutes. Add snow peas to pan and cook an additional 4-5 minutes or until peas are tender. Serve by filling lettuce bibs with meat mixture.

60

Chicken Caesar Wrap

Serves 4 Hungry College Boys
Prep Time: ~5 min
Total Time: 20 min

Ingredients

1 T olive oil
~2 lb. boneless skinless chicken breasts, cut into 1-inch
        cubes
1 t salt
1/2 t pepper
1/2 t garlic powder
9 oz. romaine lettuce, chopped
1/4 C Caesar dressing
1/2 C grated parmesan
4 large flour tortillas

Directions

Drizzle olive oil in a large pan and place on a burner on
medium-high heat. When oil is hot, add the chicken to the
pan. Season with salt, garlic powder and pepper. Stirring
occasionally cook for 10-12 minutes or until no longer pink.
Place cooked chicken in a bowl and set aside in the fridge
to chill down to room temperature. Toss the romaine
lettuce in a bowl with the Caesar dressing and grated
parmesan. Lay out tortilla and fill with chicken and salad in
the middle. Fold tortilla into a wrap. Serve cut in half.

Fresh Medley Quinoa

Serves 4 Hungry College Boys
Prep Time: ~30 min
Total Time: 50 min

Ingredients

2 C low sodium chicken broth
2 C water
2 C white quinoa
1 rotisserie chicken, shredded
1 red bell pepper, diced
1 yellow bell pepper, diced
1 cucumber, seeds removed and diced
6 green onions, chopped
9 oz. frozen spinach, cooked and drained
9 oz. grape tomatoes, halved
Dressing
Juice and zest of one lime
2 T olive oil
2 T honey
1 T pureed ginger
1/2 t salt

Directions

Combine the chicken broth and water in a large pot and place on a burner on high. Once mixture is boiling add the 2 C of quinoa and stir to combine. Reduce heat to medium-high and cook covered for 15-20 minutes. Fluff quinoa with fork and transfer it to a large bowl. Add the bell peppers, cucumber, spinach, tomatoes, green onion, and chicken to the bowl and mix to combine. In a small bowl add the lime juice, zest, olive oil, honey, ginger, and salt, whisk to combine. Pour dressing over the quinoa and toss to incorporate.

64

Chicken Parmesan Subs

Serves 4 Hungry College Boys
Prep Time: ~10 min
Total Time: 40 min

Ingredients

3 large eggs
2 C panko bread crumbs
1 T dried oregano
1 t dried basil
1 t garlic powder
1 t salt
1/2 t pepper
4 boneless skinless chicken breasts, tenderized to 1/2-inch
        thickness
24 oz. tomato sauce
1 lb. fresh whole milk mozzarella, cut into 4 large slices
4 hoagie rolls

Directions

Preheat oven to 400°. Crack the eggs in a large bowl and
whisk until beaten. In a large plate pour the bread crumbs,
oregano, basil, garlic powder, salt, and pepper and mix to
combine. Dredge each piece of chicken in egg and coat in
breadcrumbs. Press down and add as much breadcrumbs
as possible. Place the chicken in a large oven safe baking
dish and bake for 20 minutes. Remove chicken from oven
and pour sauce over chicken breast and spread with a
spoon to coat all pieces. Place one large slice of
mozzarella on top of each chicken and bake an additional
10 minutes. Slice hoagies in half and place chicken
between the two halves and serve.

66

Sheet Pan Asian Chicken over rice

Serves 4 Hungry College Boys
Prep Time: ~5 min
Total Time: 35 min

Ingredients

1/4 C brown sugar
2 T canola oil
2 t minced garlic
1 T sesame oil
Sriracha sauce
1 lb. baby carrots
1 large head of broccoli, cut into florets
4 boneless skinless chicken breasts, cut into strips
Salt
Pepper
1-1/2 C white rice
3 C water

Directions

Preheat oven to 375°. In a large bowl, combine the brown sugar, canola oil, minced garlic, sesame oil, and 2 t Sriracha sauce. Add to the bowl the carrots, broccoli, and chicken then season with salt and pepper and toss to coat. Place chicken along the middle of a greased cookie sheet and fill the perimeter of the pan with the vegetables. Pour any remaining sauce on top of the chicken and vegetables. Bake for 25 minutes and then leave in oven and turn on the ovens broil function and cook an additional 5 minutes (the heat will continue to rise while pan is inside). Pour the rice and water into a rice cooker* and turn on cooker. Serve chicken and vegetables over rice and dot with more sriracha as desired.

*For cooking without a rice cooker:
  • Cook according to package directions

Chicken Noodle Soup

Serves 4 Hungry College Boys
Prep Time: ~20 min
Total Time: 1 hour 15 min

Ingredients

Canola oil
1-3/4 lb. boneless skinless chicken thighs
Salt
Pepper
1 C onion, chopped
1 t minced garlic
10 C of reduced sodium chicken broth
1 lb. baby carrots, sliced
4 stalks of celery, chopped
2 bay leaves
1-1/2 t fresh thyme, finely chopped
12 oz. egg noodles
1 T lemon juice
1 t dried parsley

Directions

Drizzle canola oil in a large pot and place on a burner set to medium-high. Pat dry both sides of the chicken and season with salt and pepper. Allow oil to get hot, then brown smooth side of chicken for 3-4 minutes (cook in batches). Set chicken aside and reduce heat to medium and add onion to the pot. Sauté onion for 4-5 minutes scraping the brown bits off the bottom. Add garlic and cook an additional 1-2 minutes before adding the chicken broth. Add the carrots, celery, bay leaves, thyme, and chicken back to the pot and allow to simmer for 15-20 minutes or until chicken has cooked through. Remove chicken and add the egg noodles to the pot then shred chicken thighs with a pair of forks. Add the chicken back to the pot along with the lemon juice and parsley and reduce heat to low. Allow to cook covered for 20 minutes.
Remove the bay leaf and serve.

70

Curry Chicken Pitas

Serves 4 Hungry College Boys
Prep Time: ~20 min
Total Time: 50 min

Ingredients

4 boneless skinless chicken breasts
2 C red grapes, halved
1-1/2 C matchstick carrots
1/4 C sliced almonds
1/4 C fresh cilantro, chopped
1/2 C mayonnaise
1 C low-fat plain Greek yogurt
1/4 C lime juice
2 T honey
1 t salt
1/2 t red pepper flakes
3 T curry powder
1 head of romaine lettuce, chopped
8 flour pita pockets

Directions

Place the chicken breasts in the bottom of a large pot and fill the pot with water about an inch above the chicken. Place the pot on a burner set to high and allow water to boil. Once water is boiling cover the pot and reduce heat to low and cook chicken for 10-14 minutes depending on the thickness of the breast. Remove chicken and chop into bite size pieces then set aside to cool. Combine in a large bowl the grapes, carrots, almonds, and cilantro. In another bowl combine the mayonnaise, Greek yogurt, lime juice, honey, salt, red pepper flakes, and curry powder then stir to incorporate to an even consistency. When the chicken has cooled add to the bowl with the grapes, carrots, almonds, and cilantro. Combine the curry yogurt mixture with the chicken mixture and toss to mix. Fill pita pockets with curry chicken and chopped lettuce when serving.

72

Honey Mustard Chicken Wrap with Apples, Bacon, and Cheddar

Serves 4 Hungry College Boys
Prep Time: ~15 min
Total Time: 1 hour 5 min

Ingredients

4 boneless skinless chicken breasts, each cut in half
       lengthwise
8 slices of bacon
4 large flour tortillas
4 slices of cheddar, cut in half
1 large honey crisp apple, sliced thin
1 large tomato, sliced
1 head of romaine lettuce, chopped
<u>Chicken Marinade</u>
1/2 C honey mustard
1/4 C stone ground mustard
1 T apple cider vinegar
2 T apple juice
1/4 t cayenne
1/4 t smoked paprika
1/4 t garlic powder
1 t salt
1/4 t black pepper
1 t Worcestershire sauce

Directions

In a large plastic sealable bag combine the Chicken Marinade ingredients. Place the four chicken breasts in the marinade bag then close tight and shake to combine ingredients and coat chicken. Allow to marinate for 2-4 hours. Preheat oven to 400°. Line a large cookie sheet with foil and place the 8 pieces of bacon flat and separated on the cookie sheet. Bake for 15-20 minutes flipping halfway then remove from cookie sheet and allow to cool between two paper towels. Grease a cookie sheet and place the chicken breasts spaced evenly apart on the cookie sheet. Bake at 400° for 25-40 minutes depending on the size of the chicken breast or until internal

73

temperature reaches 165°. Allow chicken to rest for 2-3 minutes. Start making the wrap by placing the two halves of cheese end to end down the middle of the tortilla. Place slices of apple on top of the cheese then add tomato and lettuce. Place two slices of bacon in each wrap and top with two pieces of chicken. Close wrap and serve.

CH. 2 BEEF

76

Barbacoa Sandwiches

Serves 4 Hungry College Boys
Prep Time: ~20 min
Total Time: 8 hours 30 min

Ingredients

Canola oil
3 lb. boneless chuck roast, cut into 6 pieces
Salt
Pepper
1/2 C beef broth
1/4 C apple cider vinegar
1 lime, juiced
4 chipotle peppers in adobo, chopped
2-1/2 t minced garlic
1 T cumin
1 T dried oregano
1/4 t ground cloves
3 bay leaves
1 large loaf of French bread
4 slices baby swiss cheese
Bread and butter pickle chips
Yellow mustard

Directions

Drizzle canola oil in a skillet and turn burner to medium-high heat. Season the chuck roast pieces on all sides with salt and pepper, then brown the chuck roast pieces on all sides, about 1 minute each side. Cook pieces in batches and place in slow cooker. In a medium bowl, combine the beef broth, apple cider vinegar, lime juice, chipotle peppers, garlic, cumin, oregano, ground cloves, and bay leaves, and season with salt and pepper. Pour mixture over the meat and cook covered on low for 8 hours. Shred meat and let marinate in juice for another 10 minutes. Cut the French bread into 4 equal sections and slice horizontally. Arrange meat on bread, and top with swiss, pickles, and mustard. Brush the top of the bread with canola oil and place in a sandwich press* cooking until bread is flat and crispy and cheese has melted.

77

*for cooking on non-stick pan

- Preheat pan at medium-high heat. Place sandwich on pan and press flat with a spatula. Cook for 2-3 minutes per side. Bread should have a brown crisp edge and cheese should be melted. Watch carefully as to not burn sandwich.

Steak Fajita Quesadillas

Serves 4 Hungry College Boys
Prep Time: ~20 min
Total Time: 1 hour

Ingredients

1 t chili powder
1-1/2 t coarse salt, divided
Dash of cayenne pepper
1/4 t cumin
1/4 t garlic powder
1 T olive oil
1 onion, sliced into thin strips
8 oz. mushrooms, sliced
2 medium green bell peppers, sliced into thin strips
2 lb. NY strip steak (3 steaks), ~1/2 inch thick
1/4 t pepper
2 T canola oil
1 T butter
1 t minced garlic
4 large flour tortillas
Shredded cheddar cheese
14 oz. can corn, drained
Sour cream
Salsa

Directions

Mix together in a small bowl the chili powder, 1/2 t salt, cayenne, cumin, and garlic powder. Drizzle olive oil in a pan and place on a burner turned to medium heat. When oil is hot, add onions to pan and sauté for 2-3 minutes. Push onions to outside of pan and add mushrooms and sauté covered an additional 4-5 minutes stirring occasionally. Push all ingredients to outside of pan, add bell pepper, and cook covered for 2-3 minutes. Add spice mix to pan and stir all vegetables to incorporate. Cook for another 5-6 minutes or until peppers are tender. Set aside vegetables. Tenderize meat by jabbing both sides several times with a fork and season with 1 t salt and 1/4 t pepper. Drizzle canola oil in a nonstick pan and coat bottom of pan.

Place pan on a burner and turn heat to just below high. When oil begins to smoke place steaks in pan gently. Cook for 3 minutes and then flip and cook an additional 2 minutes. Remove pan from heat and add 1 T butter to pan and 1 t minced garlic. Lift the pan and lean it towards you so liquid pools up on the edge. Spoon butter and garlic over the steak, basting for 2 minutes. Set meat aside and let rest for 3-4 minutes. Cut steak into strips. Place quesadilla in a pan and add to half of the tortilla, cheese, steak, fajita seasoned vegetables, corn, and top with more cheese then fold in half. Cook on medium heat for 2-3 minutes per side or until cheese is melted and tortilla is crispy. Serve topped with sour cream and salsa.

82

Slow Cooker Asian Beef and Broccoli

Serves 4 Hungry College Boys
Prep Time: ~15 min
Total Time: 6-8 hours

Ingredients

2 lb. flank steak, cut into 2-inch strips
1/2 C matchstick carrots
1/2 C soy sauce
1/4 C white wine
1 t canola oil
1 t honey
1 t ground ginger
2 t minced garlic
1 t red pepper flakes
3 T brown sugar
1 t salt
1 t pepper
2 C broccoli florets, chopped
2 C water
1 C rice, dry

Directions

Place meat in the bottom of the slow cooker. In a medium bowl, mix together the carrots, soy sauce, white wine, canola oil, honey, ginger, minced garlic, red pepper flakes, brown sugar, salt, and pepper. Pour mixture over the meat and cook covered on low for 6-8 hours. One hour before serving, mix in the broccoli to the slow cooker. About 30 minutes before you are ready to serve, place water and rice into a rice cooker and start*. Serve beef and broccoli on top of rice.

*For cooking without a rice cooker:
- Cook according to package directions

84

Classic Cheeseburger

Serves 4 Hungry College Boys
Prep Time: ~10 min
Total Time: 20 min

Ingredients

Canola oil
4 1/4 lb. beef patties
Salt
Pepper
4 slices of any cheese
4 sandwich potato rolls
bread and butter pickles
1 heirloom tomato, sliced into 1/4-inch slices
1 head of romaine, chopped into sandwich size pieces

Directions

In a pan drizzle canola oil and turn burner to medium-high. Once pan is hot, salt and pepper both sides of the patties and place in the pan. Cook 4 minutes each side and place cheese on top in the last 30 seconds. Serve burger on potato rolls topped with pickles, tomato, lettuce, and any other condiment desired.

86

Slow Cooker Beef Pot Roast

Serves 4 Hungry College Boys
Prep Time: ~30 min
Total Time: 6-8 hours

Ingredients

3 stalks of celery, cut into small-medium chunks
5 large carrots, cut into small-medium chunks
1 t dried thyme
1 t dried rosemary
3 lb. boneless chuck roast
Salt
Pepper
2 T all-purpose flour, divided
2 T canola oil
8 oz. mushrooms, quartered
1/2 T butter
1 C onion, chopped
1 t minced garlic
1 T tomato paste
4 C reduced sodium beef stock

Directions

Place celery, carrots, thyme, and rosemary at the bottom of the slow cooker. Generously season both sides of the roast with salt and pepper. Sprinkle 1 T flour over the roast until coated and shake off excess. In a pan, drizzle canola oil and turn burner to medium-high heat. Brown meat on each side for 4-5 minutes or until thoroughly browned. Place roast on top of vegetables in slow cooker. Reduce heat in pan to medium, add mushrooms and butter and cook for 3-4 minutes. Add the onions and cook for another 3-4 minutes or until they are tender and begin to brown. Add garlic and stir for another minute. Stir in 1 T flour and cook for another minute, then add the tomato paste and cook for an additional minute. Slowly pour and combine the beef stock and bring to a simmer for 2-3 minutes. Pour sauce over the top of the roast and cook covered on low for 6-8 hours or until meat is tender. Skim off excess fat and serve.

88

Slow Cooker Beef Stroganoff

Serves 4 Hungry College Boys
Prep Time: ~10 min
Total Time: 6-8 hours

Ingredients

1 T olive oil
8 oz. mushrooms, sliced thick
1/4 C white wine
1-1/4 t salt, divided
3/4 t pepper, divided
2 lb. top round steak, cut into strips
3 T fresh chives, finely chopped
2 10 oz. cans cream of mushroom soup
1 t garlic powder
12 oz. egg noodles

Directions

Drizzle olive oil in a pan and turn the burner to medium heat. Sauté mushrooms for 6-8 minutes, adding the white wine, 1/4 t salt, and 1/4 t pepper about halfway through. When mushrooms are browned, set aside. Place meat in the bottom of the slow cooker then add chives, cream of mushroom, garlic powder, 1 t salt and 1/2 t pepper. Mix to combine, then cook covered on low for 6-8 hours. 20 minutes before serving, fill a pot 2/3's full of water and place on a burner on high heat. Once water is boiling, pour in the noodles and reduce heat to medium-high. Cook for 10-12 minutes or until tender. Drain the noodles and combine with the meat, stirring to incorporate.

90

"South of The Border" Burger

Serves 4 Hungry College Boys
Prep Time: ~10 min
Total Time: 45 min

Ingredients

1 medium onion, sliced into thin strips
1 T butter
4 1/4 lb. beef patties
1/8 t cayenne
1/4 t chili powder
1/4 t garlic powder
1/2 t pepper
1 t salt
1 T canola oil
4 slices pepper jack cheese
4 sandwich potato rolls
sliced jalapeños
1 beefsteak tomato, cut into 1/4-inch slices
1 head of romaine, chopped into sandwich size pieces
Chipotle ranch dressing

Directions

Place a pan on a burner at slightly less than medium heat and add onions and butter. Stir onions to coat in butter. Cook for 18-22 minutes or until onions are caramelized, stirring occasionally, then set aside. Season both sides of all patties with cayenne, chili powder, garlic powder, pepper, and salt. In the same pan used for the onions, add 1 T canola and turn the burner to medium-high. When the oil begins to sizzle or ripple, place the patties in the pan. Cook for 4 minutes per side, putting the pepper jack cheese on top in the last 30 seconds. Let burgers rest for 2-3 minutes. Dress burger by putting onions on the bottom bun, burger, a generous number of jalapeños, tomato, and lettuce on top. Spread chipotle ranch dressing on the top bun, close burger, and enjoy.

92

Hawaiian Burger

Serves 4 Hungry College Boys
Prep Time: ~15 min
Total Time: 40 min

Ingredients

8 oz. can sliced pineapple in juice, drained
1/4 t chili and lime seasoning
12 slices Canadian bacon
4 1/4 lb. beef patties
Salt
Pepper
Garlic powder
1 T canola oil
4 slices provolone
4 sandwich potato rolls
1 tomato, cut into 1/4-inch slices
1 head of romaine, chopped into sandwich size pieces
BBQ sauce

Directions

Place a pan on a burner on medium-high heat. Season pineapple slices with chili and lime seasoning. Caramelize pineapple slices for 1-2 minutes per side and set aside. Wipe out pan and reduce heat to medium. Cook Canadian bacon for 1 minute per side and set aside. Season burgers with a generous amount of salt, pepper, and garlic powder. Using the same pan add the canola oil and raise heat to medium-high. Cook burgers for 4 minutes per side, placing the cheese on top in the last 30 seconds remaining. Remove from pan and let burgers rest for 3-4 minutes. Dress burger in order: bun, tomato, burger, lettuce, Canadian bacon, pineapple, BBQ sauce, and top bun.

94

Guac Burger

Serves 4 Hungry College Boys
Prep Time: ~10 min
Total Time: 20 min

Ingredients

4 1/4 lb. beef patties
Salt
Pepper
4 slices pepper jack cheese
4 sandwich potato rolls
1 tomato, cut into 1/4-inch slices
Leaf lettuce, cut into sandwich size pieces
Guacamole:
1 medium avocado, seed removed and scooped out
1 T salsa
Pinch of salt
1 t mayonnaise
Pinch of pepper
1/2 t lime juice

Directions

In a bowl combine the avocado, salsa, salt, mayonnaise, pepper, and lime juice. Mash ingredients together to achieve a smooth consistency and set aside. *Preheat grill to 450°. Season one side of burger with salt and pepper and place seasoned side down on grates then season the other side. Cook covered for 4 minutes on each side and place cheese on in the last 30 seconds. Let burgers rest 2-3 minutes. Construct burger with bottom bun, tomato, lettuce, burger, guacamole, and top bun.

*For cooking on pan

- Add 1 T canola and turn the burner to medium-high. When the oil begins to sizzle, or smoke, place the burgers in the pan. Cook for 4 minutes per side putting the cheese on top in the last 30 seconds. Let burgers rest for 2-3 minutes.

95

96

Salisbury Steak
Serves 4 Hungry College Boys
Prep Time: ~10 min
Total Time: 40 min

Ingredients
1 T butter, divided
4 1/4 lb. beef patties
Salt
Pepper
Garlic powder
16 oz. mushrooms, cut into 1/4-inch slices
1 onion, sliced thin
18 oz. beef gravy

Directions
Place a large pan on a burner turned to medium heat.
Place 1/2 T of butter in pan and once butter is melted, add
mushrooms and sauté for 12-15 minutes or until excess
moisture has cooked off, set aside. Season top sides of
burgers with salt, pepper, and garlic powder. Place a large
pan on a burner turned to medium-high heat. Place 1/2 T
of butter in pan and once butter is melted, place the burger
seasoned side down. Season the top side of the burger
with salt, pepper, and garlic powder, and cook for 2
minutes then flip and cook an additional 2 minutes. Add
onions to the pan and rest burgers on top of the onions.
Cook covered an additional 3-4 minutes. Add the
mushrooms and gravy to the pan, reduce heat to medium-
low and let simmer for 10 minutes. Spoon gravy,
mushrooms and onions over burger when serving.

98

Beef and Barley

Serves 4 Hungry College Boys
Prep Time: ~20 min
Total Time: 8-10 hours

Ingredients

1 T butter
16 oz. cremini mushrooms, cut into 1/4-inch slices
3 lb. boneless beef chuck roast
Salt
Pepper
4 C low sodium beef broth
1 T soy sauce
1 C white wine
1-1/4 C pearl barley
1 leek, cleaned and chopped (white part only)
6 medium celery stalks, finely chopped
6 medium carrots, peeled and sliced thin
3 sprigs of fresh thyme

Directions

Add butter to a large pan on a burner at medium heat. When butter is melted sauté mushrooms for 8-10 minutes or until excess moisture has cooked off, then set aside. Season the chuck roast with salt and pepper and place in the bottom of the slow cooker. Add the beef broth, soy sauce, barley, mushrooms, white wine, leek, celery, carrots, thyme, 1 t salt, and 1/2 t pepper. Stir together ingredients then cover and cook on low for 8-10 hours. Shred beef when done cooking and serve.

100

Greek Beef Over Naan with Tzatziki

Serves 4 Hungry College Boys
Prep Time: ~10 min
Total Time: 35 min

Ingredients

Olive oil
1 C onion, chopped
Salt
Pepper
1 t minced garlic
~2 lb. lean ground beef
1 T dried oregano
~6 oz. nonfat plain Greek yogurt
1/2 t dried dill weed
1 T lemon juice
1 large cucumber, finely chopped and divided
1/2 C crumbled feta, divided
4 pieces of Naan bread, toasted and cut into quarters
1 C matchstick carrots
1 C grape tomatoes. quartered

Directions

In a large pan drizzle olive oil then add the onion with a pinch of salt and pepper and place on a burner set to medium heat. Sauté onion for 8-10 minutes stirring occasionally. Add the minced garlic and cook an additional 1-2 minutes before adding the ground beef and oregano. Season the ground beef with salt and pepper and cook for 10-12 minutes or until no longer pink then drain fat and set aside. For the Tzatziki, add in a bowl the Greek yogurt, dill weed, lemon juice, 2 T of chopped cucumber, pinch of salt, and 1 T feta, mix to combine. Serve the beef on top of the toasted Naan, then top with cucumber, carrots, tomatoes, feta, and tzatziki as desired.

Slow Cooker French Dip Sub

Serves 4 Hungry College Boys
Prep Time: ~5 min
Total Time: 8-10 hours

Ingredients

3 lb. beef chuck roast
Salt
Pepper
2 10 oz. cans reduced fat cream of mushroom soup
10 oz. can beef consommé
1 large yellow onion, halved and sliced into strips
4 hoagie rolls, sliced
8 slices provolone cheese

Directions

Season chuck roast with salt and pepper and place in the bottom of the crock pot. Empty contents of cans of cream of mushroom, beef consommé, and onion into the crock pot. Cook on Low for 8-10 hours. Shred meat when finished cooking. Place meat and juice in hoagies and top with 2 slices of provolone each then broil open-face for 3-4 minutes.

104

Sheet Pan Sausage Dinner

Serves 4 Hungry College Boys
Prep Time: ~15 min
Total Time: 1 hour

Ingredients

1-1/2 C rice
3 C water
2 lb. beef kielbasa, sliced into rounds
2 small yellow onions, cut into strips
2 green bell peppers, sliced into strips
~10 oz. grape tomatoes
1 large zucchini, cut in half and chopped
3 T olive oil
1 t dried oregano
1 t dried parsley
1/4 t smoked paprika
1 T grated parmesan
1 t salt
1/2 t pepper

Directions

Preheat oven to 400°. Pour the rice and water into a rice cooker* and turn on cooker. Place the sausage, onions, peppers, tomatoes, and zucchini on a large cookie sheet. Drizzle the olive oil then add the oregano, parsley, paprika, parmesan, salt, and pepper. Toss to combine ingredients then bake for 35-45 minutes. Serve sausage and vegetables over rice and pour any juices remaining in the cookie sheet over the top of each serving.

*For cooking without a rice cooker:

- Cook according to package directions

Slow Cooker Farmers Pie

Serves 4 Hungry College Boys
Prep Time: ~20 min
Total Time: 8-10 hours

Ingredients

~2 lb. lean ground beef
1-1/2 C onion, diced
1 lb. frozen peas
1 lb. chopped green beans
5 oz. matchstick carrots
1 t minced garlic
1 T dried oregano
1-1/2 C chicken broth
2-1/2 lb. russet potatoes, peeled and chopped
1/3 C half and half
1/4 C sour cream
Salt
Pepper

Directions

Combine in the bottom of the slow cooker the ground beef, onion, peas, green beans, carrots, garlic, oregano, chicken broth, 2 t salt, and 1/2 t pepper then stir to combine. Cover and cook on low for 8-10 hours. Place the potatoes in a large pot and fill the pot with water just above the tops of the potatoes. Place the pot on a burner set to high and once water is boiling reduce heat to medium-high and cook potatoes for 10-15 minutes or until easily pierced by a fork. Drain water from pot then add the half and half, sour cream, 2 t salt, and 1/2 t pepper to the potatoes. Mash potatoes and combine ingredients. Scoop out all the potatoes and place across the top of the meat in the slow cooker until the entire surface is covered with potatoes. Cover and cook on high an additional 30 minutes then serve.

108

Beef Lo Mein

Serves 4 Hungry College Boys
Prep Time: ~10 min
Total Time: 40 min

Ingredients

7 oz. Lo Mein noodles
1 T canola oil
~1-1/4 lb. stir fry meat (thin cut beef)
Salt
Pepper
1-1/2 C onion, chopped
1 red bell pepper, cut into thin slices
8 oz. snow peas
2 C matchstick carrots
1/4 C packed brown sugar
2 T low sodium soy sauce
1 T sesame oil

Directions

Fill a large pot about 2/3 full of water then cover and place on a burner on high. Once water is boiling add the Lo Mein noodles and cook for 8-10 minutes or until tender then drain and set aside. Drizzle 1 T canola oil in a pan and place on a burner set to medium heat. Season the beef with salt and pepper then once pan is hot, brown the stir fry meat for 2-3 minutes per side. Remove meat from pan leaving the juices and set aside. Add the onion, red pepper, snow peas, and carrots to the pan then stir to combine. Cover and steam vegetables for 5 minutes. Add the brown sugar, soy sauce, and sesame oil to the pan and stir to incorporate. Cook an additional 5 minutes uncovered stirring occasionally. Add the Lo Mein and beef to the pan and stir to combine. Cook an additional 5 minutes stirring constantly. Serve immediately.

110

BBQ Meatloaf Dinner

Serves 4 Hungry College Boys
Prep Time: ~15 min
Total Time: 1 hour 5 min

Ingredients

~2 lb. lean ground beef
1 C onion, diced
1 t minced garlic
2 large eggs
1/4 C panko breadcrumbs
1/2 C BBQ sauce, plus 2 T
1 t smoked paprika
1/2 t garlic powder
1 t salt
Pepper
~2 lb. Yukon gold potatoes, chopped into bite size pieces
1 large head of broccoli, cut into florets
Olive oil
Seasoned salt

Directions

Preheat oven to 400°. In a large bowl combine the ground beef, onion, garlic, eggs, breadcrumbs, 1/2 C BBQ sauce, smoked paprika, garlic powder, salt, and 1/2 t pepper. Mix together until evenly incorporated and form into a loaf shaped pan. Add 1-2 T of BBQ sauce on top of the meatloaf and spread across the surface. Bake for 45-50 minutes or until internal temperature reaches 160°. While the meatloaf is cooking, place the potatoes and broccoli separated on a single baking sheet. Drizzle 2 T of olive oil on the broccoli and potatoes, then season both with seasoned salt and pepper. Toss to combine ingredients. When the timer for the meatloaf is at 30 minutes place the baking sheet in the oven on the same rack. After 10 minutes, take the potatoes and broccoli out and toss to reposition then place back in the oven for the remaining 20 minutes. Allow the meatloaf to rest for 8-10 minutes then cut and serve with potatoes and broccoli.

112

The Farm Burger

Serves 4 Hungry College Boys
Prep Time: ~10 min
Total Time: 35 min

Ingredients

8 slices bacon
2 T canola oil
4 1/4 lb. beef patties
Salt
Pepper
Garlic powder
4 slices cheddar cheese
4 large eggs
4 sandwich potato rolls

Directions

Preheat oven to 400°. Line a baking sheet with foil and place 8 slices of bacon next to each other and bake for 8-10 minutes, then flip and cook an additional 6-8 minutes or until crisp. Set bacon aside between two paper towels. Drizzle canola oil in a large pan and turn heat to medium-high. Season burgers generously with salt, pepper, and garlic powder. Once pan is hot place burgers seasoned side down and season the top side with salt, pepper, and garlic powder. Cook for 4 minutes on each side and in the last 30 seconds place the 4 slices of cheddar on each of the burgers. Remove burgers from pan and allow to rest for 2-3 minutes. While burgers are resting place a non-stick pan on a burner on medium heat. Once the pan is hot, crack open 4 eggs keeping yolks intact and evenly spaced in the pan. Cook for 2-3 minutes on one side, the whites should be opaque, then flip and cook for 15-30 seconds. Remove eggs from pan and set aside delicately so not to break the yolk. Construct burger by placing the burger in the bun, then the egg, and topped with two strips of bacon.

CH. 3 PORK

Tropical Pork Tacos with Jicama Slaw

Serves 4 Hungry College Boys
Prep Time: ~45 min
Total Time: 4-6 hours

Ingredients

12 corn tortillas
Roast
1 T brown sugar
1 t salt
1/2 t pepper
1/4 t cinnamon
1/4 t garlic powder
1/4 t ground coriander
1/2 t onion powder
~3 lb. boneless pork shoulder roast
3 T barbecue sauce
20 oz. can crushed pineapple
Jicama Slaw
1/2 medium red cabbage, thinly sliced
1/2 medium jicama root, peeled and thinly sliced
6 oz. broccoli slaw
3 T fresh cilantro, chopped
3 T olive oil
3 T rice vinegar
1 fresh lime, juiced
1/2 t salt
1/4 t pepper

Directions

In a small bowl combine brown sugar, 1 t salt, 1/2 t pepper, cinnamon, garlic powder, ground coriander, and onion powder. Mix together ingredients until evenly distributed then rub onto all sides of the pork roast. Place pork in the bottom of the slow cooker. Coat outside of roast with the barbecue sauce and then empty can of crushed pineapple on top of the roast. Cook pork covered for 4-6 hours on low. In a large mixing bowl combine the cabbage, jicama, broccoli slaw, cilantro, olive oil, rice vinegar, lime juice, 1/2 t salt, and 1/2 pepper. Stir to incorporate then cover with plastic wrap and refrigerate for 3-4 hours. When pork is cooked shred the meat inside the slow cooker removing any excess fat. Serve by placing meat into corn tortillas and topping with slaw.

117

118

Black Beans and Rice

Serves 4 Hungry College Boys
Prep Time: ~20 min
Total Time: 1 hour 10 min

Ingredients

Olive oil
1 C onion, finely chopped
1 C bell pepper, chopped
1 T cumin
1 t minced garlic
2 bay leaves
2 lb. ham, cubed
2 cans black beans, 1 drained and 1 not
~14 oz. can petite diced tomatoes, drained
1/4 C apple cider vinegar
1 C water
1 C rice, any variety
Salt
Pepper

Directions

In a large pot, drizzle olive oil and toss in onion, bell pepper, cumin, garlic, bay leaves, and ham. Cook on medium-high heat, stirring often, for roughly 8-10 minutes or until onions are soft and water has mostly cooked out of the ham. Add the black beans, tomatoes, apple cider vinegar, water, and rice. Season with salt and pepper and stir to combine. Bring to a boil, then reduce heat to low. Cover and let cook for 1 hour or until rice is tender. Enjoy.

120

Slow Cooker Honey-Parmesan Pork Roast

Serves 4 Hungry College Boys
Prep Time: ~20 min
Total Time: 8-10 hours

Ingredients

8 large carrots, peeled
3 lb. boneless pork loin roast
1/3 C parmesan, grated
1/2 C honey
2 T soy sauce
1 T fresh basil, chopped
1 T dried oregano
2 T minced garlic
2 T olive oil
1/2 T salt
1/4 C chicken broth

Directions

Line the bottom of the slow cooker with the carrots and place the roast on top. In a separate bowl, combine parmesan, honey, soy sauce, basil, oregano, garlic, oil, salt, and chicken broth. Evenly cover the entire roast with parmesan mixture, cover and cook on low for 8-10 hours. When serving, spoon extra juice over individual slices for moist pork.

Dijon Mustard Pork Tenderloin

Serves 4 Hungry College Boys
Prep Time: ~10 min
Total Time: 20 min

Ingredients

2 lb. pork tenderloin, cut into 1/2-inch slices
8 oz. stone ground Dijon mustard
2 C panko breadcrumbs
Salt
Pepper

Directions

Preheat oven to 400°. Create a coating station with one bowl filled with the mustard, and in another bowl mix the bread crumbs with a generous amount of salt and pepper. Thoroughly coat each piece with the mustard then toss in the bread crumbs. Place pork on a greased baking sheet and bake for 8 minutes, flipping after 4 minutes.

124

Monte Cristo

Serves 4 Hungry College Boys
Prep Time: ~10 min
Total Time: 35 min

Ingredients

2 lb. brown sugar glazed ham, sliced
2 T mayonnaise, divided
8 slices challah bread, divided
8 slices gouda cheese, divided
8 T strawberry jelly
1/4 C powdered sugar, divided

Directions

Preheat oven to 350°. Tightly wrap the ham in foil and place in an oven-safe pan filled with a 1/4 C of water in the bottom. Bake for 30 minutes. Spread mayonnaise on one side of each slice of bread. On the side without mayonnaise, stack ham, spread 1-2 T of jelly, cover with two slices of cheese, then add another small stack of ham and close with other slice of bread (mayonnaise should be on the outside of the sandwich). Place in Panini maker* mayonnaise side touching the burners. Cook 4-5 minutes or until brown and crispy. Serve by dusting with powdered sugar.

*for cooking on non-stick pan

- Preheat pan with burner at medium-high heat. Place sandwich on pan and press flat with a spatula. Cook for 2-3 minutes per side. Bread should have a brown crisp edge and cheese should be melted. Watch carefully as to not burn sandwich.

126

Apricot and Rosemary Pork Tenderloin

Serves 4 Hungry College Boys
Prep Time: ~10 min
Total Time: 30 min

Ingredients

3 T olive oil, divided
4 t minced garlic, divided
1 t salt
1/2 t pepper
3 T dried rosemary
2 1 lb. pork tenderloins
1 C apricot preserves
3 T lemon juice

Directions

Preheat oven to 425°. In a bowl combine the 2 T olive oil, 3 t garlic, salt, pepper, and rosemary. Spoon mixture onto the pork and rub to coat thoroughly. Drizzle 1 T olive oil in a pan and turn the burner to medium-high heat. When the oil begins to smoke, brown the pork on all sides for a total of 4 minutes. Place pan in oven and bake for 15 minutes. In a bowl combine the apricot, lemon juice, and 1 t garlic. After finished baking, spoon apricot mixture over both tenderloins until thoroughly covered. Place back in oven for 10 minutes or until internal temperature reads 160°. Remove pork from oven and continuously baste with pan juices while it rests for 5 minutes.

128

Slow Cooker Pork Tenderloin and Grilled Broccoli

Serves 4 Hungry College Boys
Prep Time: ~10 min
Total Time: 4 hours

Ingredients

2 1 lb. pork tenderloins
1 envelope dry onion soup mix
3/4 C red wine
1 C water
3 T soy sauce
1-1/2 T minced garlic
4 stalks of broccoli, stems peeled, sliced into thirds
	lengthwise
1/4 C olive oil
1/4 t pepper
1/2 t salt

Directions

Place the pork, soup mix, wine, water, soy sauce, and garlic in a slow cooker and cook covered on low for 4 hours. Place the broccoli flat sides down on a grill tray. In a small bowl, mix the olive oil, salt, and pepper. Preheat grill to 350° and place tray on grates. Brush broccoli with olive oil mixture and cook covered for 6 minutes. Open lid and cook 4 more minutes brushing with oil. Flip each piece and brush once more then cook covered an additional 2-3 minutes or until there is a slight char. To serve pork, spoon juices from slow cooker over the meat.

130

Cinnamon Apple Pork Chops

Serves 4 Hungry College Boys
Prep Time: ~10 min
Total Time: 30 min

Ingredients

2 T butter
4 pork loin chops, ~1-inch thickness and 2 lb. total
Salt
Pepper
2 medium Honeycrisp apples, cored and sliced thin
1 medium onion, sliced thin
2 T brown sugar
2 t cinnamon
Dash of cayenne
2/3 C apple cider
1/3 C heavy cream

Directions

Heat a pan on medium-high heat and add butter.
Generously season both sides of the pork chops with salt
and pepper. When the butter is melted, brown the pork
chops for 3 minutes each side. Remove from pan and set
aside. Toss in apples and onions and reduce heat to
medium. Sauté for 10-12 minutes, stirring occasionally,
being sure to scrape all the brown bits off the bottom of the
pan. Add in the brown sugar, cinnamon, and cayenne,
and stir to combine. Cook for an additional 2-3 minutes
then add the apple cider and heavy cream, mixing to
combine. Add the pork back to the pan, giving space so
the meat is in contact with the pan and only sauce is
underneath the pork. Pour apple mixture over the top of
each chop and cook for 4 minutes each side or until
internal temperature reaches 145°. Let meat rest for 5
minutes. Serve by pouring apple mixture on top of the
pork.

132

Slow Cooker Honey-Lime Ginger Pork Tenderloin with Chili-Lime Rice

Serves 4 Hungry College Boys
Prep Time: ~15 min
Total Time: 8 hours

Ingredients

1/2 C honey
1/4 C soy sauce
1 T Worcestershire sauce
Juice and zest of one lime
1 t minced garlic
1 T pureed ginger
1/2 t salt
1/4 t pepper
2 1 lb. pork tenderloins
1 C rice, dry
1 C water
1 C chicken broth
1 t chili-lime seasoning

Directions

In a bowl stir to combine the honey, soy sauce, Worcestershire, lime juice and zest, garlic, ginger, salt, and pepper. Place pork at the bottom of the slow cooker and pour honey mixture evenly over the pork. Cook covered on low for 8 hours, flipping halfway. In the last half hour of cooking, begin cooking rice. In a rice cooker* add the rice, water, chicken broth, and chili-lime seasoning. Stir to combine and start rice cooker. Remove pork from slow cooker and shred. Save juice from bottom of slow cooker. Serve pork on top of rice and spoon juices over top.

*For cooking without a rice cooker:
- Cook according to package directions

134

Slow Cooker Hawaiian Pork Sliders

Serves 4 Hungry College Boys
Prep Time: ~10 min
Total Time: 8-10 hours

Ingredients

~3 lb. boneless pork shoulder roast
1/2 C BBQ sauce
20 oz. can pineapple chunks in juice
1 package honey-wheat Hawaiian rolls 12-count, sliced
6 slices of provolone, cut in half
Dry-rub
1 T coarse sea salt
1 t garlic powder
1 t smoked paprika
1 t cumin
1 t black pepper
1 t chili powder
1/4 t cayenne pepper

Directions

The night before, mix in a bowl the dry rub: salt, garlic powder, smoked paprika, cumin, black pepper, chili powder and cayenne. Rub the spice mix over the entire roast then cover and refrigerate until ready to cook the next day. Before cooking, add the barbecue sauce and juice from the can of pineapple (save the chunks) in a bowl and whisk to combine. Place roast in the bottom of the slow cooker and pour sauce over the roast. Cover and cook on low for 8-10 hours. Shred pork inside slow cooker removing any excess fat. Serve by placing pork on Hawaiian rolls then top with provolone and pineapple chunks.

135

Ham and White Bean Soup

Serves 4 Hungry College Boys
Prep Time: ~15 min
Total Time: 1 hour 10 min

Ingredients

2 T olive oil
1-1/2 C onion, chopped
3 medium carrots, peeled and diced
4 celery stalks, diced
2 lb. brown sugar glazed ham, cubed
2 t minced garlic
2 bay leaves
4 C vegetable broth
4 C chicken broth
1 t dried thyme
1 T dried parsley
1 t cumin
1 t salt
1/2 t pepper
2 15 oz. cans of cannellini beans, drained

Directions

In a large pot drizzle olive oil and toss in the onion, carrots, and celery. Sauté on medium heat for 8-10 minutes stirring occasionally. Add the ham, garlic, bay leaves, vegetable broth, and chicken broth to the pot and turn the heat to high. Once a rolling boil is reached, reduce heat to medium and cook covered 25 minutes. Reduce heat to low and add in the thyme, parsley, cumin, salt, and pepper. Cook covered an additional 30 minutes. Finally, add in the cannellini beans and cook uncovered 5 more minutes.

Slow Cooker Peach Pork Chops Over Rice

Serves 4 Hungry College Boys
Prep Time: ~10 min
Total Time: 8-10 hours

Ingredients

1/2 C reduced sodium chicken broth
2 T apple cider vinegar
1 T packed brown sugar
1/4 t red pepper flakes
1 red onion, sliced thin
4 fresh peaches, pitted and sliced thin
4 boneless pork loin chops
Salt
Pepper
3 large sprigs fresh thyme
1-1/2 C rice
3 C water

Directions

Add the chicken broth, apple cider vinegar, brown sugar, red pepper flakes, onion and peaches in the bottom of the slow cooker and stir to incorporate. Season both sides of the pork chops with salt and pepper and nestle pork underneath all the ingredients. Add the 3 sprigs of thyme and cook covered on low for 8-10 hours flipping the pork chops halfway. Remove thyme from the slow cooker. Pour the rice and water into a rice cooker* and turn on cooker. Serve Pork and other ingredients over rice and spoon juice over the top.

*For cooking without a rice cooker:
- Cook according to package directions

140

Ham and Tomato Grilled Cheese with Tomato Basil Soup

Serves 4 Hungry College Boys
Prep Time: ~10 min
Total Time: 25 min

Ingredients

Mayonnaise
8 slices of butter bread
8 slices of sharp cheddar cheese
2 large tomatoes, cut into 8 slices and chop remaining
    tomato
2 1/2 lb. ham steaks, cut in half
2 19 oz. cans of tomato basil soup

Directions

Spread mayonnaise on the outside of every slice of bread.
Then dress sandwich layering cheddar, tomatoes, ham,
then cheddar again and close the sandwich. Empty
contents of cans of soup and remaining chopped tomato in
a sauce pan and cook for 12-15 minutes on medium
stirring occasionally. Place a nonstick pan on a burner set
to medium heat. Once pan is hot, place two sandwiches in
the pan. Press sandwiches or use a heavy object to
compress sandwiches and cook for 3-4 minutes per side.
Cut diagonally and serve with soup for dipping.

142

Pork Marsala

Serves 4 Hungry College Boys
Prep Time: ~25 min
Total Time: 50 min

Ingredients

1 C all-purpose flour, plus 1 T
Salt
Pepper
2 lb. pork tenderloin, cut into 1/2-inch medallions
Olive oil
Butter
1 lb. mushrooms, cut into thick slices
3 T shallots, minced
1 T minced garlic
2/3 C marsala cooking wine
1-1/4 C half and half

Directions

In a bowl combine 1 C flour, 1 T salt, and 1/2 t pepper and mix to evenly combine. Cover the pork in flour mixture and shake off excess flour. Drizzle 1 T olive oil and 1 T butter in a large pan on medium-high heat. Once pan is hot, brown the pork for 3-4 minutes per side (cook in batches) and then set aside. Reduce heat to medium and add the mushrooms to the pan and sauté for 5-7 minutes. Add the shallots, garlic, and 1 T olive oil. Cook and stir 1-2 minutes before mixing in 1 T of flour cooking for an additional 1-2 minutes. Deglaze pan with marsala wine and cook liquid down for about 3-4 minutes stirring intermittently. Add the half and half to the pan and let simmer for 5-6 minutes stirring occasionally. Reduce heat to low and allow sauce to thicken up. Pour sauce over pork when serving.

144

Slow Cooked Ribs with Mashed Potatoes and Coleslaw

Serves 4 Hungry College Boys
Prep Time: ~25 min
Total Time: 4 hour 30 min

Ingredients

2 ~3 lb. packages baby back ribs
Salt
Pepper
1/4 C honey
Rib Sauce
19 oz. BBQ sauce
1/4 C brown sugar
4 T apple cider vinegar
1 T Worcestershire sauce
1 T chili powder
1 T cayenne pepper
1 t garlic powder
3 T dried oregano
Coleslaw
16 oz. coleslaw cabbage
1/2 C coleslaw dressing
Mashed potatoes
4 medium russet potatoes, peeled and chopped into 1-inch
        pieces
2 t salt
1 t pepper
2 T unsalted butter
1/4 C sour cream
1/4 C whole milk or cream

Directions

Cut ribs into thirds and season both sides generously with salt and pepper. In a bowl combine rib sauce: BBQ sauce, brown sugar, apple cider vinegar, Worcestershire, chili powder, cayenne pepper, garlic powder, and oregano and whisk to incorporate. Place rib sections inside the slow cooker and pour sauce mixture over each piece, coating entirely. Cover and cook on high for 4 hours. For

145

coleslaw, empty contents of cabbage into a large bowl and toss with coleslaw dressing. Place potatoes in a large pot and fill with water until just above all potatoes. Turn burner to high and once water is boiling cook for 10-12 minutes or until fork tender. Drain water then mash potatoes. Add salt and pepper as well as butter, milk, and sour cream. Stir together until creamy. After ribs have cooked for 4 hours, preheat oven to broil. Remove ribs from slow cooker and place on a baking sheet. In a small bowl, combine 1/2 C of the juices from the slow cooker with the honey. Pour honey mixture over the top of all the ribs and then broil for 5 minutes.

CH. 4 PASTA

148

Knock off Pasta Carrabba

Serves 4 Hungry College Boys
Prep Time: ~25 min
Total Time: 1 hour

Ingredients

Olive oil
1 T minced garlic
4 boneless skinless chicken breasts, chopped into 1-inch
      cubes and seasoned with salt and pepper
8 oz. angel hair pasta
8 oz. mushrooms, quartered
1/4 C white cooking wine
Salt
Pepper
15 oz. basil pesto alfredo sauce
15 oz. can sweet peas, drained
Grated parmesan
Dried parsley

Directions

Drizzle olive oil in a pan and turn burner to medium-high heat. Toss in garlic and chicken, and brown for 6-8 minutes, stirring occasionally. Set chicken and all juices aside and reduce heat to medium. Toss in mushrooms to brown for 1-2 minutes then deglaze with the white wine and season with salt and pepper. Sauté for 5-7 minutes, stirring often, then add back the chicken mixture. Pour in the sauce and allow to simmer on low for 12-15 minutes, adding in the peas at the last minute. Fill a large pot about 2/3 full of water and place on a separate burner on high. Add a small drizzle of olive oil and 1 t salt to the water. When the pot reaches a rolling boil, add the pasta and reduce heat to medium-high, cooking for 5-7 minutes or until tender. Drain the pasta and return to pot. Combine all ingredients into the pot and mix to combine. Serve topped with parmesan and parsley.

150

Creamy Cheddar and Smoked Sausage Penne

Serves 4 Hungry College Boys
Prep Time: ~10 min
Total Time: 30 min

Ingredients

Olive oil
2 lb. smoked turkey sausage, cut into 1/2-inch rounds
1 C onion, diced
1 t minced garlic
2 C chicken broth
14 oz. can diced tomatoes
1-1/2 C whole milk, divided
16 oz. penne pasta
1 C (4 oz.) shredded sharp cheddar, divided

Directions

In a large pan, drizzle olive oil and turn burner to medium heat. Brown sausage and sauté onions for 8-10 minutes. Add garlic and cook for another minute. Add chicken broth, tomatoes, 1 C milk and pasta. Raise heat to high and stir to combine. Once boiling, stir constantly, scraping the bottom to avoid sticking, for 10 minutes. Reduce heat just below medium when most of the liquid has cooked down, add the remaining 1/2 C of milk, and continue cooking and stirring for 3-5 more minutes until pasta is tender. Remove from heat and mix in 3/4 C of cheddar. Once cheese is thoroughly combined, top with remaining cheddar and allow to melt.

152

Spinach and Sausage Stuffed Shells

Serves 4 Hungry College Boys
Prep Time: ~5 min
Total Time: 1 hour 30 min

Ingredients

1 lb. Italian sausage, remove from casing
1 lb. turkey sausage, remove from casing
12 oz. jumbo pasta shells
4 C ricotta cheese
4 t garlic powder
1 t oregano
2 C (8 oz.) shredded mozzarella cheese, divided
3/4 C grated parmesan
2 large eggs
9 oz. frozen spinach, thawed and drained
24 oz. tomato sauce

Directions

Preheat oven to 350°. In a pan, brown the sausages on medium-high heat for 8-10 minutes. Drain fat and crumble sausage, set aside. Fill a large pot 2/3 full of water and bring to a boil. Fill a large bowl with ice water. Once water reaches a rolling boil add the jumbo shells and cook for 10 minutes or until just pliable. Drain pasta and place into ice water to stop cooking process. In a large mixing bowl, combine the ricotta, garlic powder, oregano, 1 C of mozzarella, parmesan, eggs, 1/2 the sausage, and spinach, mixing well. In a 9x13 oven-safe baking dish, coat the bottom with tomato sauce. Stuff the shells to max capacity and place in sauce. Top with the remaining sausage and 1 C of mozzarella. Bake for 30 minutes, rotating the dish after 15 minutes. Let cool for 10 minutes and serve.

154

Angel Hair with Spicy Vodka Sauce

Serves 4 Hungry College Boys
Prep Time: ~10 min
Total Time: 40 min

Ingredients

2 lb. smoked turkey sausage or smoked pork sausage,
    sliced into 1/2-inch rounds
1 T olive oil
3 shallots, finely grated
1-1/2 T minced garlic
1 t salt, divided
1/4 t pepper
1/2 t dried oregano
1/4 t dried red pepper flakes
24 oz. vodka sauce
1 T hot sauce
1 C grape tomatoes
8 oz. angel hair pasta

Directions

Place a large pan on a burner on medium-high heat.
When pan is hot, brown sausage for 6-8 minutes then set
aside. Reduce heat to medium and add olive oil. Toss in
shallots and garlic and season with 1/2 t salt, pepper,
oregano, and red pepper flakes. Sauté for 3 minutes
scraping all the brown bits off the bottom. Add vodka
sauce, hot sauce, sausage, and grape tomatoes stirring to
combine. Reduce heat to medium-low or low and let
simmer for 20 minutes stirring occasionally. Fill a large pot
2/3 full of water, add 1/2 t salt, and a few drops of olive oil,
and place on a burner set to high. When water is boiling
add in pasta and reduce heat to medium-high. Cook pasta
uncovered stirring occasionally for 6-8 minutes or until
tender. Empty pasta into a colander and drain excess
water. Add pasta to sauce and stir to combine.

156

Taco Bake

Serves 4 Hungry College Boys
Prep Time: ~10 min
Total Time: 1 hour

Ingredients

16 oz. bow tie pasta
1 T olive oil
1 onion, chopped
2 lb. lean ground beef
16 oz. salsa
14 oz. can diced tomatoes with chilis
2-1/2 C (10 oz.) shredded cheddar, divided
1 T chili powder
1/4 t dried oregano
1/4 t garlic powder
1 t cumin
1/8 t cayenne
1 t salt
1/2 t pepper
2 C tortilla strips
Sour cream

Directions

Preheat oven to 350°. Place a large pot filled 2/3 with water on a burner on high and bring to a boil. Cook pasta according to package directions then drain and set aside. In a large pan add olive oil and sauté onions for 6-7 minutes on medium heat. Push onions to outside of pan and add ground beef. Brown beef for 10-12 minutes or until no longer pink. Drain excess fat then add the salsa, diced tomatoes, 1-1/2 C cheddar, chili powder, oregano, garlic powder, cumin, cayenne, salt, and pepper. In a greased 9x13 mix to combine the bow tie pasta and meat mixture, and bake covered with foil for 20 minutes. Remove from oven and top with the tortilla strips and 1 C of cheddar. Bake uncovered for 10 minutes. Serve topped with a dollop of sour cream.

158

Rotini Alfredo with Ham, Mushrooms, Peas, and Onion

Serves 4 Hungry College Boys
Prep Time: ~20 min
Total Time: 1 hour

Ingredients

16 oz. tri-color rotini pasta
1 T olive oil
1-1/2 lb. glazed ham, cubed
3/4 C onion, diced
1/4 t salt
1/8 t pepper
8 oz. white mushrooms, cut into 1/4-inch slices
15 oz. frozen peas
15 oz. alfredo sauce

Directions

Fill a large pot 2/3 full of water then add a small drizzle of olive oil and 1 t salt to the water. Place on a burner turned to high. When the pot reaches a rolling boil, add the pasta and cook according to package directions then drain and set aside. In a pan drizzle olive oil and add ham, cook on medium-high for 10-12 minutes. Remove ham from pan and add to pot with drained pasta, leave juices in pan. Reduce heat to medium and add onion to pan, season with salt and pepper. Sauté for 8-12 minutes or until onions begin to caramelize, stirring occasionally. Move onions to outside edge of pan and add mushrooms. Cook mushrooms for 8-10 minutes or until browned and excess moisture has cooked off, stir occasionally. Add frozen peas to pan and stir to combine ingredients let cook for 1-2 minutes then add alfredo sauce to pan. Mix to incorporate ingredients into sauce and allow to simmer for 5-8 minutes. Combine ingredients from sauce pan into the pot with pasta then mix to coat pasta in sauce.

160

Lemon Butter Angel Hair with Chicken

Serves 4 Hungry College Boys
Prep Time: ~10 min
Total Time: 45 min

Ingredients

4 boneless skinless chicken breasts
1 t salt
1/2 t pepper
1/4 t garlic powder
2 t dried oregano, divided
4 pats of butter
8 oz. angel hair pasta
2 T dried parsley
1 T butter, melted
1 t minced garlic
1/4 C grated parmesan
3 T lemon juice
2 T olive oil

Directions

Preheat oven to 400°. Season both sides of the chicken with salt, pepper, garlic powder, and dried oregano. Place chicken breast smooth side up on a greased baking sheet and place a pat of butter on top of each piece of chicken. Bake chicken for 25-40 minutes depending on size of the breast or until internal temperature reaches 165°. Fill a large pot about 2/3 full of water and place on a separate burner on high. Add a small drizzle of olive oil and 1 t salt to the water. When the pot reaches a rolling boil, add the pasta and reduce heat to medium-high cooking for 5-7 minutes or until pasta is tender. Drain pasta and return to pot. Toss in parsley, 1 t oregano, melted butter, minced garlic, parmesan, lemon juice, and oil. Stir to combine ingredients seasoning with salt and pepper to taste. When chicken is fully cooked let rest for 2-3 minutes then chop into bite size pieces and serve on top of pasta. Top with grated parmesan when serving.

161

162

Pepper Jack Bacon Mac and Cheese

Serves 4 Hungry College Boys
Prep Time: ~15 min
Total Time: 45 min

Ingredients

8 strips of bacon
16 oz. small shell pasta
4 T butter
1/4 C flour
2-3/4 C whole milk, warmed in microwave
1-1/2 C (6 oz.) white cheddar cheese, freshly grated
1-1/2 C (6 oz.) pepper jack cheese, freshly grated
1 t salt
1/2 t pepper
1/2 t dried mustard powder
1/4 t cayenne

Directions

Preheat the oven to 400°. Tightly wrap foil around an edged cookie sheet and place bacon spread apart on foil. Bake for 15-20 minutes in the lower third of the oven, flipping the slices halfway. Remove the bacon and place between paper towels to cool. Crumble the bacon or finely chop it and set aside for later (save 1 t of bacon bits for topping). Fill a large pot about 2/3 full of water and place on a burner on high. Add a small drizzle of olive oil and 1 t salt to the water. When the pot reaches a rolling boil, add the pasta and reduce heat to medium-high cooking for 12-15 minutes or until tender then drain and return to pot off the burner. Place a medium sauce pan on a burner set to medium heat. Melt butter then add the flour whisking constantly for 3-4 minutes or until a golden yellow roux has formed. Slowly whisk in the milk and allow to boil, whisking throughout and scraping the bottom. Whisk in the cheese handfuls at a time and add the bacon, salt, pepper, mustard, and cayenne. Continue to cook whisking for 10-12 minutes or until sauce is creamy and coats the back of a spoon. Add sauce to the pasta and combine. Serve topped with crumbled bacon.

163

164

Ham and Asparagus Carbonara

Serves 4 Hungry College Boys
Prep Time: ~15 min
Total Time: 35 min

Ingredients

8 oz. angel hair pasta
Olive oil
1 C onion, diced
Salt
1 t minced garlic
2 lb. ham, cubed
1 bundle of asparagus, last 2 inches of bottom removed
Pepper
4 large eggs
1 C heavy cream
1 C (4 oz.) shredded parmesan

Directions

Preheat oven to 400°. Fill a large pot about 2/3 full of water, 1/2 t salt, and a few drops of olive oil and place on a burner set to high. Once water is boiling add the pasta and cook for 6-8 minutes or until tender, drain and return to pot and set aside. Place a pan on medium heat and drizzle 1 T olive oil and add in the onion and a pinch of salt. Sauté onions for 12-15 minutes or until onions are a caramel color then reduce heat to medium-low. Add the garlic to the pan and sauté for an additional 1-2 minutes stirring occasionally. Add the ham to the pan and stir to combine. Let ham cook about 5-6 minutes stirring occasionally. Cut asparagus into thirds and place on a cookie sheet then drizzle with olive oil and season with salt and pepper and stir to combine. Spread asparagus out on the cookie sheet and bake for 12 minutes. In a large mixing bowl whisk to combine the eggs, cream, parmesan, 1/2 t salt and a sprinkle of pepper. Place pot of pasta back on a burner on medium-low and add the ham mixture as well as the asparagus and mix to combine. Pour in the cream mixture to the pot and toss to combine for about 3

minutes so that the eggs and cream cook. Serve
immediately.

Chicken Penne with Sun Dried Tomato Alfredo

Serves 4 Hungry College Boys
Prep Time: ~10 min
Total Time: 1 hour

Ingredients

16 oz. penne pasta
4 boneless skinless chicken breasts
1/2 t fine salt
1/4 t pepper
1/4 t onion powder
1/8 t paprika
1/4 t dried oregano
1 T olive oil
1 t minced garlic
3 C fresh spinach, roughly chopped
1/4 C sundried tomatoes packed in oil, chopped
15 oz. parmesan alfredo sauce
Grated parmesan

Directions

Fill a large pot 2/3 full of water, then add a small drizzle of olive oil and 1 t salt to the water. When the pot reaches a rolling boil, add the pasta and reduce heat to medium-high, cooking for 12-15 minutes or until tender, then drain and set aside. *Preheat grill to 450°. Season both sides of the chicken with salt, pepper, onion powder, paprika, and oregano. Place chicken smooth side down on the grates and cook for 5-7 minutes per side or until internal temperature reaches 165°, then let rest for 2-3 minutes. In a pan drizzle olive oil and place on a burner at medium heat. When oil is smoking add garlic to pan and sauté for 1-2 minutes, then add the spinach and sun dried tomatoes. Sauté for 6-8 minutes or until all spinach is wilted. Add sauce to pan and mix to combine. Let simmer for 8-10 minutes stirring occasionally. Cut chicken into bite size pieces and add to pot with pasta. Pour sauce into pot with pasta and chicken and mix to coat chicken and pasta. Serve topped with grated parmesan.

*For cooking on pan

- Add 1 T olive oil and turn the burner to medium-high. When the oil begins to sizzle, or smoke, place the chicken in the pan. Cook for 6-8 minutes per side or until internal temp reaches 165°.

169

170

Chicken Fettuccini Alfredo

Serves 4 Hungry College Boys
Prep Time: ~10 min
Total Time: 35 min

Ingredients

8 oz. fettuccini pasta
1 T olive oil
4 boneless skinless chicken breasts, cubed
Salt
Pepper
2 t dried oregano
1 stick unsalted butter
2 t minced garlic
1-1/2 T flour
2 C heavy cream
1/2 C (2 oz.) shredded parmesan cheese

Directions

Fill a large pot about 2/3 full of water, 1/2 t salt, and a few drops of olive oil and place on a burner set to high. When water is boiling add the pasta and reduce heat to medium-high. Cook pasta for 12-15 minutes or until tender then drain and set aside. In a separate pan drizzle the olive oil on medium-high heat. Season the chicken with 1 t salt, 1/4 t pepper, and 2 t oregano. Once pan is hot, add chicken to the pan and cook for 6-8 minutes or until cooked through, stirring occasionally. Remove pan from heat and set aside. Place a sauce pan on a burner on medium heat and melt the stick of butter. Once butter is melted add garlic and whisk together for 1 minute. Add 1/4 t of salt and a pinch of pepper to the sauce. Slowly whisk in the flour for 3-4 minutes then whisk in half of the cream until evenly combined then whisk in the other half of the cream. Allow for sauce to thicken stirring occasionally to keep from sticking to the bottom of the pan. Whisk in 1/2 C of parmesan and stir until combined. Add pasta back to the large pot and combine with the sauce and chicken. Stir to combine ingredients and serve.

171

CH. 5 OTHER

Flatbread Personal Pizza

Serves 4 Hungry College Boys
Prep Time: ~10 min
Total Time: 20-22 min

Ingredients

Traditional
4 large flatbreads
1-1/2 lb. bag frozen meatballs, cooked
1 C tomato sauce, divided
1/2 oz. fresh basil, julienned and divided
2 C (8 oz.) shredded mozzarella, divided

BBQ chicken
4 large flatbreads
1 BBQ rotisserie chicken, shredded and divided
1 C BBQ sauce, divided
1/2 C red onion, sliced thin and divided
2 C (8 oz.) shredded mozzarella, divided
Blue cheese crumbles

Cheeseburger
4 large flatbreads
1-1/2 lb. ground beef, cooked and divided
1 C tomato sauce, divided
1/2 C yellow onion, chopped and divided
2 C (8 oz.) shredded cheddar, divided
1/2 C relish, divided

Philly
4 large flatbreads
1-1/2 lb. sirloin, cooked and cut in strips, divided
1 C Cheese Whiz, divided
1 C yellow onion, sliced thin and divided
1 C bell pepper sliced thin, divided
8 oz. mushrooms sliced, divided

Buffalo chicken
4 large flatbreads
1 original rotisserie chicken, shredded and divided
1 C buffalo sauce, divided
1/2 C red onion, sliced thin and divided
Blue cheese crumbles

White (vegetarian)
4 large flatbreads
9 oz. frozen chopped spinach, defrosted and drained
1 C alfredo sauce, divided
1 C ricotta cheese, divided
2 C (8 oz.) mozzarella, divided
Season with salt and pepper

Directions

Preheat oven to 400°. Place flatbread on a greased baking sheet. Spread sauce, then spread meat evenly across flatbread. Arrange cheese and toppings as desired. Bake pizzas for 10-12 minutes or until cheese is melted and bubbling. Let cool for 2-3 minutes. Cut as desired and enjoy.

176

Taco Salad

Serves 4 Hungry College Boys
Prep Time: ~15 min
Total Time: 45 min

Ingredients

Olive oil
1 C yellow onion, finely chopped
2 lb. ground turkey or lean ground beef
16 oz. can seasoned red beans
8 oz. can of corn, drained
3 T salsa
1/2 T cumin
1/2 T chili & lime seasoning
1/2 T garlic powder
1/2 T salt
1/2 T pepper
9 oz. spring mix lettuce
1 C grape tomatoes, quartered
1 C matchstick carrots
Sour cream
Mild salsa
2 C (8 oz.) four cheese Mexican blend
1 bag tortilla strips

Directions

Drizzle olive oil on a pan and turn burner to medium heat. Sauté onion for 8-10 minutes then push to the outside edge of the pan and add meat to the pan. Brown meat for 6-8 minutes. Drain 2/3 of the liquid and return to heat. Add beans (and all liquid), corn, 2 T salsa, cumin, chili & lime, garlic, salt, and pepper to the pan and mix to combine. Reduce heat to medium-low, and allow to simmer for 15-20 minutes, stirring occasionally. Evenly divide the spring mix, tomatoes, and carrots onto four plates as meat simmers. Serve by topping the salad with the meat mixture, a dollop of sour cream, a few scoops of salsa, sprinkle of cheese, and several tortilla strips.

Breakfast for Dinner Quiche

Serves 4 Hungry College Boys
Prep Time: ~25 min
Total Time: 1 hour 20 min

Ingredients

1 lb. turkey sausage, remove from casing
1/2 C onion, chopped
8 oz. mushrooms, sliced
1/2 C bell pepper, chopped
20 oz. shredded hash browns, (thawed if frozen)
Butter
Salt
Pepper
1/3 C grape tomatoes, finely chopped
1 T fresh chives, chopped
6 large eggs
1/2 C heavy cream
1/2 C (2 oz.) shredded cheddar

Directions

Preheat oven to 400°. Brown sausage on medium-high heat for 6-8 minutes, stirring frequently, then drain and set aside. Lower to medium heat and sauté the onions, mushrooms, and bell pepper for 6-8 minutes. Set aside vegetables and let cool. Evenly arrange hash browns in a large oven-safe pan. Place several small dots of butter on top of the potatoes, then season with salt and pepper. Prebake for 10 minutes or until edges brown. Arrange sausage, onions, mushrooms, tomatoes, and chives on top of the potatoes. In a large mixing bowl, combine the eggs, cream, cheese, salt, and pepper, and pour in the pan. Bake for 25 minutes or until a knife in the center comes out clean. Let cool for 3-5 minutes and enjoy.

Meatball Marinara

Serves 4 Hungry College Boys
Prep Time: ~15 min
Total Time: 30 min

Ingredients

1-1/2 lb. frozen meatballs, divided
1 large loaf French bread, divided
2 C (8 oz.) shredded mozzarella, divided
2 C marinara sauce, divided

Directions

Cook meatballs according to package directions. Preheat oven to 400°. Cut the French bread into 4 equal sections, then slice each section in half. Remove some bread from center of each section to make room for all ingredients. Spoon marinara onto each slice of the bread and pile on the meatballs. Top with more sauce and cover with mozzarella. Bake for 8-10 minutes on a baking sheet or until bread is crisp and cheese is melted. Add as much cheese or sauce as desired and enjoy.

182

Slow Cooker Sloppy Joe

Serves 4 Hungry College Boys
Prep Time: ~10 min
Total Time: 4 hours

Ingredients

1 T olive oil
1 C onion, chopped
1 green bell pepper, chopped
3 lb. ground turkey or ground beef
12 oz. tomato paste
2 t yellow mustard
2 T brown sugar
1 t garlic powder
1 t salt
1 t pepper
4 potato rolls

Directions

Drizzle olive oil in a pan and turn the burner to medium heat. Sauté the onions and peppers for 10-12 minutes or until translucent and tender. Pour contents into slow cooker. In the same pan, brown the meat for 10-12 minutes or until all meat is no longer pink. Add meat to slow cooker. Add the tomato paste, mustard, brown sugar, garlic powder, salt, and pepper to the slow cooker. Mix and incorporate all ingredients together. Cover and cook on low for 4 hours. Serve on potato rolls.

Sweet Potato Soufflé

Serves 4 Hungry College Boys
Prep Time: ~10 min
Total Time: 50 min

Ingredients

3 large sweet potatoes, peeled and chopped
1/2 C evaporated milk
1/2 C sugar
1 t vanilla extract
2 large eggs
1/3 stick of butter
1/2 t salt
Topping
1/2 C brown sugar
1 C pecans chopped, divided
1/3 C all-purpose flour
1/3 stick of butter, melted

Directions

Preheat oven to 350°. Put sweet potatoes in a large pot
and fill with water until just above potatoes. Turn burner to
high and boil water. Once it reaches a boil, reduce to
medium-high heat and cook 8-10 minutes or until easily
pierced by a fork. Drain water from pot and mash sweet
potatoes until smooth. Add in the evaporated milk, sugar,
vanilla, eggs, butter, and salt. Mix until fluffy and stiff
peaks form, then pour contents into a 9x9 casserole dish
or equivalent. In a bowl combine the brown sugar, 1/2 C
pecans, flour, and butter until even consistency. Sprinkle
topping over sweet potatoes and sprinkle the remaining
pecans over the top. Bake for 35 minutes uncovered.

186

Wysocki Stuffing

Serves 4 Hungry College Boys (Enough for two meals)
Prep Time: ~20 min
Total Time: 1 hour

Ingredients

1 lb. sage sausage, remove from casing
5-6 stalks of celery, chopped
1-1/2 C onion, chopped
14 oz. herbed stuffing mix
1 medium granny smith apple, finely diced
1-1/2 t poultry seasoning
2 large eggs
2 C chicken broth

Directions

Preheat oven to 350°. In a large pan, brown sausage on medium-high heat for 10-12 minutes. Set sausage aside. In the same pan reduce heat to medium and cook the celery and onion for 10-12 minutes or until tender. In a large mixing bowl combine the stuffing mix, sausage, celery, onion, apple, poultry seasoning, eggs, and chicken broth. Mix to combine. Place in greased 9x13 and bake 30 minutes covered in foil and 5 minutes uncovered until edges brown.

188

Green Bean Casserole

Serves 4 Hungry College Boys
Prep Time: ~15 min
Total Time: 50 min

Ingredients

2 lb. fresh green beans, chopped into bite size pieces and
    cooked until tender
10 oz. can cream of mushroom soup
3/4 C evaporated milk
1 t Worcestershire sauce
1/8 t pepper
1-1/3 C fried onions, divided

Directions

Preheat oven to 350°. In an oven-safe dish combine the green beans, soup, milk, Worcestershire, pepper, beans, and 2/3 C fried onions. Bake for 30 minutes. Stir, then top with remaining 2/3 C fried onions and bake an additional 5 minutes.

190

Ham, Spinach, and Cheddar Breakfast Bake

Serves 4 Hungry College Boys
Prep Time: ~10 min
Total Time: 45 min

Ingredients

5 oz. Italian seasoned croutons
1 lb. ham, cubed
9 oz. chopped frozen spinach, thawed and drained
1 C (4 oz.) shredded sharp cheddar
1 C (4 oz.) Italian blend cheese
10 large eggs
1-1/2 C half-and-half
1/2 t salt
1/2 t pepper

Directions

Preheat oven to 350°. Grease an oven-safe 9x13 casserole dish or equivalent. Lay croutons, ham, spinach, and both cheeses along the bottom of the dish. In a mixing bowl whisk the eggs then add the half-and-half, salt, and pepper. Pour egg mixture over the top of crouton base. Bake for 40-45 minutes or until eggs are firm and edges are lightly browned.

Slow Cooker Jambalaya

Serves 4 Hungry College Boys (Enough for two meals)
Prep Time: ~25 min
Total Time: 6 hours

Ingredients

3 boneless skinless chicken breasts, cubed
14 oz. andouille sausage, sliced into 1/2-inch rounds
2 C fresh okra, sliced into 1/2-inch rounds
1 red bell pepper, chopped
1 green bell pepper, chopped
1 yellow bell pepper, chopped
1 orange bell pepper, chopped
1 C onion, chopped
1 t minced garlic
1 T creole seasoning
14 oz. can diced tomatoes
2 T hot sauce
2 bay leaves
5 C reduced sodium chicken broth
1-1/2 C rice
3 C water

Directions

Add all ingredients except water and rice into the slow cooker and cook covered on low for 4-6 hours. Pour the rice and water into a rice cooker* and turn on cooker. If jambalaya has too much liquid, cook uncovered on high for 30-45 minutes. Toss rice in slow cooker and stir to combine. Remove bay leaves and serve.

*For cooking without a rice cooker:

- Cook according to package directions

194

Neapolitan Pizza

Serves 4 Hungry College Boys
Prep Time: ~10 min
Total Time: 35 min

Ingredients

4 12" personal pizza crusts
1 C tomato sauce
1 lb. fresh whole milk mozzarella, cut into small chunks
        and divided
1/2 oz. fresh basil leaves, quartered and divided

Directions

Preheat oven to crust package directions. Pour 1/4 cup of
tomato sauce onto each crust and spread evenly. Place
1/4 of the mozzarella and spread across each pizza.
Arrange 1/4 of the basil leaves onto each pizza. Bake
according to package directions or until cheese is melted
and bubbly. Cut and serve.

Low Country Boil Foil Packets

Serves 4 Hungry College Boys
Prep Time: ~35 min
Total Time: 50 min

Ingredients

4 ears of corn, cut into thirds
1 lb. andouille sausage, sliced into thin rounds
1-1/2 lb. large shrimp, peeled and deveined
2 lb. baby red potatoes, quartered
4 T olive oil, divided
2 t Old Bay seasoning, divided
1/2 t salt, divided
1/4 t pepper, divided
4 12-inch sheets heavy duty aluminum foil
Dried parsley

Directions

Preheat grill* to 450°. Place 3 pieces of corn, 1/4 of the sausage, 1/4 of the shrimp, 1/4 of the potatoes in the center of each aluminum foil sheet. Drizzle 1 T olive oil and season with 1/2 t old bay, 1/8 t salt, and a few cranks of fresh ground pepper for each packet. Incorporate ingredients and fold edges closed air tight to allow to steam inside pack. It is important to have an airtight seal, or they will not steam properly. Place packets on grill and cook for 12-15 minutes. Serve garnished with parsley.

*For cooking in oven
- Preheat oven to 425° and bake for 25-30 minutes

198

Slow Cooker Swedish Meatballs with Rice

Serves 4 Hungry College Boys
Prep Time: ~10 min
Total Time: 4-5 hours

Ingredients

10 oz. can cream of mushroom soup
2 C beef broth
1 t garlic powder
1 T Worcestershire sauce
Pinch of cayenne
1/2 t salt
1/2 t pepper
2 lb. frozen meatballs
1 C sour cream
1-1/2 C white rice, dry
3 C water

Directions

In the slow cooker, whisk together cream of mushroom soup with beef broth until evenly combined. Add in garlic powder, Worcestershire, cayenne, salt, and pepper. Whisk to combine ingredients then add meatballs stirring until all are covered in sauce. Cook covered on high for 4 hours. Add in the sour cream after 4 hours, mix to combine, and cook covered an additional 30 minutes. Pour the rice and water into a rice cooker* and turn on cooker. Serve meatballs over rice and ladle extra sauce on top when serving.

*For cooking without a rice cooker:
  • Cook according to package directions

200

Open Face Fried Egg Sandwiches

Serves 4 Hungry College Boys
Prep Time: ~5 min
Total Time: 10 min

Ingredients

1 T butter
8 large eggs
Salt
Pepper
8 pieces of Canadian bacon
8 slices of cheddar cheese
4 plain bagels, sliced in half and toasted

Directions

Place butter in a pan on medium heat. When butter is melted and bubbling crack 4 eggs into the pan and season with a pinch of salt and pepper. Cook for about 2 minutes when whites are opaque and flip all eggs. For runny eggs cook about 15-20 seconds after flipped, for hard-fried cook another 1-2 minutes. Place a medium pan on medium-high heat with 4 pieces of Canadian bacon. Cook 1-2 minutes per side. Repeat process for eggs and Canadian bacon for a second batch to make a total of 8 open face sandwiches. Serve by placing cheese on the bagel first then followed by the Canadian bacon and topped with the egg.

202

Broccoli Cheddar Soup

Serves 4 Hungry College Boys
Prep Time: ~20 min
Total Time: 1 hour

Ingredients

2 C low sodium chicken broth
1 large head of broccoli, chopped
1 C onion, finely chopped
2 t minced garlic
1 bay leaf
1 C matchstick carrots
3 T unsalted butter
3 T flour
2 C half and half
1/4 t cayenne
1/4 t dried basil
1/4 t ground allspice
1/4 t garlic powder
1/4 t salt
1/4 t pepper
2 C (8 oz.) aged white cheddar, freshly grated

Directions

In a medium pot add the chicken broth, 2/3 of the chopped broccoli, onion, garlic, bay leaf, and carrots then stir to incorporate. Cook covered on medium-high heat for 15 minutes or until vegetables are tender. After the vegetables are cooked, drain them and reserve the liquid. In a separate large pot, melt the butter over medium heat. Add flour and whisk for 3-4 minutes until a golden roux has formed. Remove the bay leaf from the pot and add reserved liquid from the vegetables to roux and whisk to combine. Slowly pour and whisk in 2 C of half and half then add the cayenne, basil, allspice, garlic powder, salt, and pepper. Continue whisking and add the cheddar to the pot. Once the cheese has melted, add the cooked vegetables and stir to combine. Toss in the remaining broccoli and reduce heat to low and let simmer for 10 minutes stirring occasionally.

Ultimate Pizza

Serves 4 Hungry College Boys
Prep Time: ~20 min
Total Time: 1 hour

Ingredients

Olive oil
16 oz. mushrooms, cleaned and sliced
Salt
Pepper
1 yellow onion, sliced thin
1 green bell pepper, sliced thin
1 lb. Italian sausage, remove from casing
2 12" pizza crusts
1/2 C tomato sauce, divided
1-1/2 C (6 oz.) Italian cheese blend, divided
1-1/2 C (6 oz.) shredded mozzarella, divided
6 oz. pre-sliced pepperoni

Directions

Drizzle olive oil in a large pan on medium heat. Add the mushrooms to the pan, season with salt and pepper and sauté for 6-8 minutes, stirring occasionally and then set aside. Using the same pan, add the onions and bell pepper and cook for 6-8 minutes, stirring occasionally then set aside. While the onions and peppers cook, place another pan on a burner on medium-high heat and cook the Italian sausage for 10-12 minutes or until no longer pink then crumble and set aside in a large paper towel lined bowl to absorb some of the excess fat. Preheat the oven to 400°. Place pizza crusts on a baking sheet. Spoon a 1/4 C of tomato sauce across the entire surface of the pizza crust. Then evenly top each pizza with 3/4 C of Italian blend cheese and 3/4 C of mozzarella. Top each pizza with half of the crumbled sausage. Divide all the vegetables in half and top each pizza evenly with half of the vegetables. Top the pizza with as much pepperoni as desired and brush the outsides of the crust with olive oil. Bake for 10-14 minutes or until cheese has melted and edges of vegetables have crisped up.

206

Hawaiian Pizza

Serves 4 Hungry College Boys
Prep Time: ~10 min
Total Time: 20 min

Ingredients

2 12"premade pizza crusts
1/2 C tomato sauce, divided
4 C (16 oz.) shredded mozzarella, divided
6 oz. Canadian bacon, chopped
20 oz. can pineapple chunks, drained and divided

Directions

Preheat oven according to crust package directions. Pour 1/4 C tomato sauce on each pizza crust and spread to evenly coat the entire surface leaving about 1/2-inch of crust without sauce along the outside. Sprinkle mozzarella evenly across both pizzas then top with half of the Canadian bacon and pineapple on each pizza. Place pizzas on a baking sheet and bake according to package directions. Cut into desired number of pieces and serve.

208

Foil Packet Sweet Potatoes 4 Ways with Grilled Zucchini

Serves 4 Hungry College Boys
Prep Time: ~15 min
Total Time: 20 min

Ingredients

4 small sweet potatoes, peeled and cut into 1/2-inch cubes
4 8-10 inch wide sheets of foil
6 zucchinis, cut lengthwise in thirds cutting off both ends
1 T olive oil
1 T Montreal Steak seasoning mix
Plain Sweet Potato
1/8 t salt
Pinch of pepper
1 t olive oil
Sweet Potato Pie
1/8 t cinnamon
Dash of nutmeg
Dash of ginger powder
1/8 t brown sugar
1/8 t vanilla
1 t olive oil
Savory Herb Sweet Potato
1/8 t salt
Pinch of pepper
1/2 t herbes de provence
1 t olive oil
Southwest Sweet Potato
1/8 t cumin
Dash of paprika
1/8 t salt
Pinch of pepper

Directions

Preheat grill to medium heat or about 400°. Place
chopped sweet potatoes in the center of each sheet of foil
then add ingredients for specific potato variation and mix to
combine. Fold packet closed so potatoes are fully
enclosed with no air escaping and place on back burners

of grill cooking for 15-20 minutes. Pat dry the slices of zucchini then drizzle with olive oil evenly coating. Sprinkle Montreal steak seasoning on top of zucchini. Place zucchini oil side down. Grill for 5 minutes then flip and cook an additional 5 minutes. Remove foil packets and zucchini from grill and serve.

CH. 6 DESSERTS

Candy Bar Pumpkin Cookies

Serves 4 Hungry College Boys (~18 cookies)
Prep Time: ~20 min
Total Time: 30 min

Ingredients

3/4 C dark brown sugar
6 T unsalted butter, softened
1 large egg
1/2 C pumpkin puree
1/2 t vanilla extract
1/2 C flour
1 C quick oats
3/4 t cinnamon
1/8 t ground ginger
1/8 t ground nutmeg
1/4 t ground cloves
1/4 t baking powder
1/4 t baking soda
1/2 t salt
3 fun-size Twix, finely chopped
3 fun-size Milky Way, finely chopped

Directions

Preheat oven 350°. Mix together the brown sugar, butter, egg, pumpkin, and vanilla until uniform consistency. In a separate bowl mix flour, oats, cinnamon, ginger, nutmeg, cloves, baking powder, baking soda, and salt. Slowly add dry ingredients to wet and mix until combined. Add chopped chocolate candies and fold in. Use a tablespoon measure to shape and portion dough on a greased cookie sheet with cookies 1-2 inches apart. Bake for 10-12 minutes and cool on a wire rack. Do not overcook; the cookies will stiffen up as they cool.

214

Wysocki Pumpkin Pie

Serves 4 Hungry College Boys
Prep Time: ~10 min
Total Time: 1 hour

Ingredients

Sprinkle of all-purpose flour
1 refrigerated pie crust
15 oz. can pumpkin puree
1-1/4 C heavy cream
2/3 C sugar
3 large eggs, divided
1 t ground cinnamon
1/2 t ground nutmeg
1/2 t vanilla extract
1/4 t salt
Whipped cream

Directions

Preheat oven to 425°. Sprinkle a 9-inch pie plate with flour. Lay out dough pushing crust down and towards the edges then crimp tops of edges with fingers. Pierce pie dough several times across bottom and sides with fork. Pre-bake for 10 minutes. In a large mixing bowl combine the pumpkin, cream, sugar, 2 eggs, cinnamon, nutmeg, vanilla and salt. Whisk until an even consistency throughout. Beat remaining egg and brush the edges of the crust then sprinkle sugar on edges. Preheat oven to 350°. Pour pumpkin mixture into crust and bake for 50-60 minutes. The edges should be set but still jiggly in middle. Let cool completely or chill overnight. Serve topped with whipped cream.

216

Wysocki Pecan Pie

Serves 4 Hungry College Boys
Prep Time: ~15 min
Total Time: 20 min

Ingredients

Sprinkle of all-purpose flour
1 refrigerated pie crust
1 C packed brown sugar
1/3 C melted butter
3/4 C light corn syrup
1 t vanilla extract
1/2 t salt
3 eggs
1-1/2 C pecan halves
Whipped cream

Directions

Preheat oven 425°. Sprinkle a 9-inch pie plate with flour. Lay out dough pushing crust down and towards the edges. Crimp tops of edges with fingers. Pierce pie dough several times across bottom and sides with fork. Pre-bake for 10 minutes. In a large mixing bowl combine the brown sugar, butter, corn syrup, vanilla, salt, and eggs. Whisk together ingredients then stir in pecans. Preheat oven to 350 °. Bake 35-45 minutes. If edges are browned after 20 minutes cover with foil. Pie should be set and not jiggly. Let cool 30 minutes and chill 2 hours or overnight. Serve topped with whipped cream.

Homemade Turtle Brownies

Serves 4 Hungry College Boys
Prep Time: ~10 min
Total Time: 55 min

Ingredients

1-1/4 C granulated sugar
5 T unsalted butter melted
2 large eggs
1 egg yolk
1 t vanilla extract
1/3 C vegetable oil
3/4 C unsweetened cocoa powder
1/2 C all-purpose flour
1/8 t baking soda
1 T Cornstarch
1/4 t salt
1 C walnuts chopped, plus 1 T
6 T caramel topping

Directions

Preheat oven to 325°. Line an 8x8 nonstick baking dish with foil and generously butter the sides and base of the foil in the pan. In a large mixing bowl whisk to combine the sugar, melted butter, eggs, egg yolk, vanilla extract and vegetable oil. In another large mixing bowl stir to combine the cocoa powder, flour, baking soda, cornstarch, and salt. Add about half of the dry ingredients to the wet and stir to combine. Once homogenous add the rest of the dry ingredients and stir to combine. Add the walnuts to the batter and mix to incorporate. Pour half of the batter into the foil-lined pan and spread out across the entire bottom. Drizzle 3 tablespoons of caramel topping over the batter then pour the rest of the batter in and spread until level. Drizzle remaining caramel on top and add 1 t chopped walnuts. Take a knife and drag it through the batter in a zig-zag motion until caramel is mixed throughout the batter. Bake for 40-45 minutes. Brownies will be done when a toothpick stuck through to the bottom comes out clean.

220

Banana Bread

Serves 4 Hungry College Boys
Prep Time: ~15 min
Total Time: 1 hour 30 min

Ingredients

1/2 C packed dark brown sugar
1/2 C granulated sugar
1/2 t vanilla extract
1/2 C butter, softened
2 large eggs
4 overripe medium-large bananas, mashed
1-1/2 C flour
1/2 t salt
1 t baking soda
3/4 C chopped walnuts

Directions

Preheat oven to 350°. In a large mixing bowl cream together the brown sugar, granulated sugar, vanilla extract, and butter. In another bowl crack both eggs and add the 4 mashed bananas, mix until combined. Add the banana mixture to the butter and sugar and mix to combine. In a bowl combine the flour, salt, and baking soda and give a quick stir. Combine dry ingredients with wet and stir until combined. Add in walnuts and give a few stirs to the batter. Do not over mix. Butter then flour the inside of a loaf pan covering all the sides and bottom. Pour the batter into the loaf pan and bake for 1 hour and 15 minutes or until a toothpick stuck through the middle comes out clean. Once cooled cut and serve immediately or completely wrap tight in plastic wrap and let chill in fridge overnight.

Key Lime Pie

Serves 4 Hungry College Boys
Prep Time: ~5 min
Total Time: 20 min

Ingredients

3 egg yolks
14 oz. can sweetened condensed milk
1/2 C fresh lime juice
10" graham cracker crust
1 t lime zest
Whipped cream

Directions

Preheat oven to 350°. In a mixing bowl whisk together the egg yolks, condensed milk, and lime juice. Whisk together thoroughly until even consistency. Pour the mixture into the pie crust and even out until level. Bake for 15 minutes and allow to cool for 10 minutes. Cover and refrigerate overnight. Add whip cream to the entire border of the pie crust and sprinkle the lime zest along the top of the whip cream. Cut and serve.

Pineapple Upside Down Cake

Serves 4 Hungry College Boys
Prep Time: ~10 min
Total Time: 55 min

Ingredients

1/2 C canola oil
3 large eggs
~15 oz. box supermoist yellow cake mix
2 20 oz. cans of pineapple slices in juice (reserve 1 C juice
      and cut slices in half)
4 T butter
1/2 C packed brown sugar
Maraschino cherries
1/4 C pecan halves

Directions

Preheat oven to 350°. In a large mixing bowl add the vegetable oil, eggs, cake mix, and pineapple juice and mix using a whisk for 2-3 minutes or until evenly combined. In a 10-inch or 12-inch cast iron skillet melt the 4 T of butter over medium heat then add the brown sugar to the pan and stir to combine with the butter. Raise heat to medium-high and allow brown sugar mixture to bubble for 1-2 minutes. When the sugar is bubbling arrange pineapple slices on the bottom of the pan and around the entire edge of the pan. In the empty spaces add maraschino cherries and pecans. Slowly and evenly add the cake batter to the pan and bake for 40 minutes. The top should be a golden brown and a toothpick should come out clean. Let skillet rest and cool for 10-12 minutes then loosen the edge of the cake by running a knife around the outside. Place a heat safe plate or dish on top of the cake and press together the plate and the skillet to flip. Once flipped, slowly lift skillet off then cut and serve.

226

Slow Cooker Chocolate Lava Cake

Serves 4 Hungry College Boys
Prep Time: ~10 min
Total Time: 3-4 hours

Ingredients

~15 oz. box devil's food cake mix
3-1/4 C whole milk, divided
3 large eggs
1/2 C canola oil
~4 oz. package instant chocolate pudding
1 C dark chocolate morsels
Whipped cream

Directions

Grease the bottom and sides of the crock pot. In a large mixing bowl combine the devil's food cake mix, 1-1/4 C whole milk, eggs, and canola oil. Whisk together ingredients for 2 minutes until even consistency with no lumps. Pour cake mixture into the crock pot. In a mixing bowl combine the pudding mix and 2 C of whole milk. Whisk together for 2 minutes until an even consistency and pour directly into the center of the cake batter. Do not mix ingredients together. Sprinkle over the top of the entire cake 1 C of dark chocolate morsels. Cook covered on low for 3-4 hours. Scoop out and serve and (optional) top with whipped cream.

Made in United States
Troutdale, OR
10/09/2024

23613973R00143